Afternoon Tea

*A History and Guide to the
Great Edwardian Tradition*

Vicky Straker

AMBERLEY

For Olivia and Mats

All recipe photography courtesy of the author.

First published 2015

Amberley Publishing
The Hill, Stroud
Gloucestershire, GL5 4EP

www.amberley-books.com

British Library Cataloguing in Publication Data.
A catalogue record for this book is available from the British Library.

ISBN 978 1 4456 5031 9 (paperback)
ISBN 978 1 4456 5032 6 (ebook)

Typeset in 10pt on 13pt Sabon.
Typesetting and Origination by Amberley Publishing.
Printed in the UK.

Contents

Why Tea?

Rumour has it that the ritual of afternoon tea was inadvertently introduced in the 1840s by the 7th Duchess of Bedford. Finding that she had a 'sinking feeling' of hunger between the hours of lunch and dinner, tea with a dainty of some sort was brought to her boudoir. If the ritual of entertaining friends over tea in Belvoir Castle and London was to be discovered, she feared ridicule; much to her surprise it was not long before the idea caught on and soon became an observed everyday interlude.

Prior to this, tea had been drunk at different times of the day, diarised by Thomas Turner, '1756 Monday 16th August – We came away about three o'clock, and called at my Aunt Ovendean's, drank tea and came home about 8.35.' There are countless further examples including a letter requesting a parent to send some tea to Eton. Tea was more commonly taken after dinner until the 1840s, though exactly when it became an afternoon ritual is debatable. An unfinished novel by Jane Austen suggests that afternoon tea may have been taken as early as 1804.[1]

According to legend, tea was discovered in China around 2700 BC when leaves from a camellia tree fell into fresh water being boiled by a servant of Emperor Shen Nung. Tea is seen in Greek and Roman texts as well as the Bible, in which Methuselah, who apparently lived for a thousand years, never partook in the consumption of hot drinks. Drinking too many, it was thought, warmed the blood to the extent that it was associated with hot rivers of Hell! Some said that the length of time it took the biblical figure Rachel to conceive may be blamed on the hot liquors she drank which, it was thought, may also have lead to her hot temper.[2]

The Portuguese bought tea from China in 1557. It is therefore no surprise that tea drinking was influenced by Portuguese Catherine of Braganza, wife of King Charles II, who introduced it to the English Royal Court in 1662, from where it infiltrated. This infiltration may have been gradual indeed as it is thought that the crate of tea which formed part of Catherine's dowry may have been sold by the Court to alleviate royal debt, so high was its value. The Queen's fondness of the drink is illustrated in a poem written in 1663 by Edmund Waller in her honour for her birthday:

Venus her Myrtle, Phoebus has his bays;
Tea both excels, which she vouchsafes to praise.
The best of Queens, the best of herbs, we owe
To that bold nation which the way did show
To the fair region where the sun doth rise,
Whose rich productions we so justly prize.
The Muse's friend, tea does our fancy aid,
Regress those vapours which the head invade,
And keep the palace of the soul serene,
Fit on her birthday to salute the Queen. 3

Among the emotions evoked by tea, English traveller and philanthropist Jonas Hanway wrote in 1758 that working-class women drinking tea were 'neglecting their spinning knitting etc spending what their husbands are labouring hard for, their children are in rage, gnawing a brown crust, while these gossips are canvassing over the affairs of the whole town, making free with the good name and reputation of their superiors'.

Dr Samuel Johnson, English writer and moralist, a self-confessed 'hardened and shameless tea-drinker', published a satirical essay in response, detailing his absolute pleasure in tea drinking, which brought comfort to his midnights and mornings. Arguing that the Navy would not be supplied with tea if it meant 'bilious and nervous sailors, instead of hearts of oak, and sinews of iron', he concluded that tea, even if not enjoyed by all, was an excuse to gather together and 'prattle'.4

Tea Temperance was studied in the mid-1700s by which time John Wesley, founder of the Methodist movement, recommended its abstinence, advising that what would have been spent on tea could be given to the poor. Not drinking hot drinks formed part of religious abstinence, as well as his early opinion that it brought about 'Paraytick (paralytic) disorder'. Despite this advice, in later life Wesley returned to tea drinking, though at times it may have been a herbal infusion of mint or sage, and, with religious self-denial, was only drunk in sensible and infrequent quantities.

Ironically, in the nineteenth century, when alcohol was affecting the productivity of the working classes, Wesley's Methodist church encouraged abstinence from alcohol through the drinking of tea!

With positive influences shown by royalty, the aristocracy, and an eminent writer (among I am sure, others) the way was paved for us to embrace tea. Following the Duchess of Bedford's ritual, by the second half of the nineteenth century drinking tea, accompanied by nibbles, had become tea-time, the fourth meal of the day.

The Chinese, who originally used tea as a medicinal drink, had the monopoly on export to Britain until the British East India Tea Company finally started importing tea in 1669, having tried and failed to do so in 1619. A battle with the Dutch over the spice trade had taken over with Great Britain being on the losing side. Until 1669, tea reached British shores on English-registered ships, the tea having been exported by the Dutch.5 The British Empire started tea production on a large scale in Assam, India in the mid-1800s when land had been offered to a European who would cultivate tea with a view to exporting it. An Indian nobleman ended up with the task, and succeeded admirably, forming a relationship with the British East India Tea Company.

The British planted tea on the island of Ceylon, now known as Sri Lanka, after a blight on coffee leaves devastated the crops in 1869. Cocoa beans having failed, tea was the solution to this destruction, and soon Ceylon had become a major tea producer. By 1900 India had 4,000 tea estates, Ceylon 2,000. Over 50 per cent of Britain's tea came from India, 30 per cent from Ceylon, and just 7.5 per cent each from both China and Indonesia.[6]

Tea is thought to have been used in India since ancient times, though possibly under a different name, so this is speculative. It was not until the 1920s that tea became a regular part of Indian lifestyle; previously it was only known to have been drunk by Anglo-Indians. Now India exports only 30 per cent of its tea, the remainder being drunk at home. Several tea plants were grown and blended according to taste. Some were made for a particular person such as Earl Grey, British Prime Minister in the 1830s, others were named after where they come from or even a time of day, such as English Breakfast Tea, which combines leaves from Assam, Ceylon and Kenya.

The East India Tea Company was the only legal importer of tea to Great Britain. Having the monopoly, they kept their profits higher than they needed to, so that with the additional tax imposed by the UK government, its cost was prohibitive. With tea smuggling becoming commonplace, much of it would not go through customs or have anything to do with the East India Tea Company. Officers employed to oversee the transport of tea by the East India Tea Company also profited by using space within their cabin on board the ship to hide tea leaves, which they would smuggle and sell at their own profit.[7]

Tea was so light that it was an easy commodity to smuggle. The majority of tea drunk in Great Britain was brought in by smugglers who were able to sell it without its excessive tax. The smugglers were usually coastal-based, and it is thought that this enabled the spread of tea drinking through the social orders as well as to the countryside from cities and towns. The aristocracy and upper classes took their tea to their country houses, but were most likely unaware that the labourer next door was sipping his own cup of tea, bought at a vastly reduced price.

Despite the knowledge of many that smuggling had its dark side, tea was so popular that it continued to be smuggled. This popularity did not correspond with import records, which were not increasing despite tea's growing popularity, due to the high quantities of tea reaching many of its drinkers though surreptitious means.

The reprehensibility of tea smuggling may sound forgivable in light of the greed of the East India Tea Company and high tax placed on it by the government. Men who would otherwise have been employed in agriculture, as chimney sweeps, jehus (carriage drivers) or other such useful jobs may be tempted away to become tea smugglers, such was the lure of profit. However, the unscrupulous methods of some of the smuggling gangs shine horrific light on what illegal profiteering can do. In 1747, the tea smuggling Hawkshurst gang were about to have evidence given against them in Chichester.

Two men, travelling to give evidence in court, stopped in a public house as a rest stop during their journey, only to find two more smugglers in the pub who knew of their destination. The men due to give evidence were cruelly put to death in a long and slow slaughter. Eight ringleaders of the gang were sentenced to death, but in no way as cruel an end as that imposed on their victims.[8]

The loss of profit of the East India Tea Company lead them to being in debt to the British government. Due to the smuggling efforts, it also had a surplus of tea. In order to raise some of the funds it owed, permission was gained from the British government to export to America, thus levying a tax of three shillings per pound on tea to be exported. Although this was less than the charge on tea imported to Britain, America objected to any charge at all, feelings being fraught that a country so far away, whose government did not have jurisdiction over them, should be paid any levy at all. Smuggling contributed to the Boston Tea Party in 1773. This protest against duty on tea meant tea was tipped overboard into the harbour, rather than brought onto shore. Far-reaching consequences, more suited to a history book than a tea book, of this 'Boston Tea Party' played a part in the American War of Independence which culminated in America becoming a self-governing nation, rather than a group of British Colonies.[9]

The tax on tea was reduced to 12.5 per cent from 119 per cent by William Pitt when he became prime minister at the very young age of twenty-four. The deficit was made up with increased window tax, which explains why blocked windows are seen today in old houses, a consequence of their owner's attempts to reduce their tax bill. Tea smuggling ceased almost immediately, the profit margin no longer reaping the same financial rewards. With smuggling having led to the spread of drinking tea to the middle and working classes, so much was drunk that the profit made by reduced tax combined with window tax meant that it was not long before the Exchequer was in a sound financial position.[10]

Teatime had become such an institution that by the 1860s university life and schooling involved instruction in its art. Outside of studying, a girl at Girton College, Cambridge described there being 'an ample margin for tennis, walks and other amusements, and also for social intercourse – tea parties being the favourite form of this latter.' By 10.30 p.m. 'disturbing noises, such as piano playing' had to stop. The art of tea parties was taught alongside learning how to remove stains, test for fresh eggs, and arrange laundry and other such housewifely duties.[11]

It had become fashionable to have tea breaks, and employers began to allocate periods of time during the working day for their employees. Part of servants' pay included a tea allowance. However, this was not always the case, as during the Victorian and Edwardian era, some of the aristocracy and the upper classes were of the opinion that the privilege of taking a break for a cup of tea should be reserved for them alone. Another issue to face was that the long term effects of tea drinking were not known, and could possibly cause harm to their servants. In households and businesses where employers were not impeded by this view, tea continued to grow as a part of daily breaks.

The habit of taking tea started with low tea which was a light snack between lunch and dinner typically consisting of sandwiches, cakes, biscuits and scones, all of which were served in a delicate manner at about four o'clock in the afternoon. High tea, which was more substantial and replaced dinner, involved meat, bread and other more ample dishes. The difference lay in high tea being for workers who when their day was finished, would need replenishment soon after. This would therefore be eaten later than low tea, when they were working, and earlier than dinner, by which time they would have become too hungry to wait, explaining why supper or dinner is sometimes called tea. Low tea was generally had by those who did not work, and high tea by those who did. 'High' and 'low' are used because low tea was served on comfortable low chairs in a drawing room, and high tea was served at a kitchen table using upright 'high' chairs.[12]

Dorothy Hartley writes that good food was more easily procurable in the countryside where produce was plentiful and, as Bee Wilson writes, 'a "big slice of solid cake" as against some dull "tea and biscuits" in the city' were more likely to be found. Fillings for sandwiches were varied in the countryside and likely to involve fresh vegetables, straight from harvest where seasons were clearly marked.[13]

Smoking opium was popular, British sailors having introduced it in the 1840s; it was referred to as the 'absinth of women' by Alexandre Dumas, the French writer. By the Edwardian era, the British Medical Journal wrote of its disapproval of morphine tea parties. These generally took place among the upper classes. Ladies would sit down to tea, dismiss the servant, lock the door, and inject their arms in turn, offering more if more was desired. So widespread was this habit that those who could afford it had silver and gold syringes made by jewellers.[14] Ether and marijuana were had by some, strawberries being soaked in ether and eaten, as well as being drunk with water or brandy. Cocaine also played a part, known as the 'wonder drug' by Sigmund Freud, until it was later restricted when its side effects were acknowledged. The first international drug control treaty, the International Opium Convention, was signed in The Hague in 1912.

On 22 January 1901, when Queen Victoria died after a sixty-three-year reign, Edward stopped being Prince of Wales, a title he had held for the longest time in history to that date. Not only was he now monarch of the United Kingdom, but Emperor of India, the British Empire and British Commonwealth until his death on 6 May 1910. The empire had widened during the Victorian era to include Canada, Australia, Pakistan, India, Malta, Ceylon, New Zealand, Newfoundland, South Africa and the Irish Free State. Despite the Crown's influence having greatly lessened towards the end of the seventeenth century, it still had more sway then that it does today.

Behind the scenes Queen Victoria tried to influence Parliament in their choice of ministerial appointment and subsequent running of the country. Her descent into the depths of mourning following the death of her husband, Prince Albert, in 1861, lead to a period of withdrawal which only changed slightly in the latter years of her reign. To her people she was a paragon of moral virtue, looked up to as the grandmother of the country. Having enjoyed parties and embraced a social life with her husband Albert when he was alive, it was not long before this was forgotten, so that her son's enjoyment of the good life was something with which she felt unable to relate.

Edward's calendar each year involved travel for both entertainment and relaxation. This ranged from shooting and deer stalking in Albergeldie near Balmoral, the London Season at Marlborough House in The Mall, July at Cowes' Regatta on the Isle of Wight, the winter at Sandringham, followed by a few weeks in Biarritz on the French Riviera. At about the end of July, in a perhaps vague attempt at losing some weight put on during all this fun, (King Edward's waistline measured in at forty-eight inches, and his nickname was 'Edward the Wide') Edward spent some time at Marienbad or Karlsbad spas in western Czechoslovakia.

Prince Edward was born in 1841, so that by the time he became an adult, the habit of taking tea had become widespread. Edward met and became engaged to Princess Alexandra of Denmark in 1861; the marriage taking place in 1863. His mother was not wholly happy with this match, the Danes in her opinion being 'those fast Christians'.[15] Alexandra did cartwheels as a child, smoked a hookah and ate with her fingers on a visit to Egypt in 1869. She was described as drawing gasps of admiration at her enchanting good looks and was perhaps a good match in not being a wilting flower, considering the caddish behaviour of her husband.[16] During Prince Edward's engagement he conducted an affair with an Irish actress, Nellie Clifden, under the all-seeing eyes of fellow officers while in army training. And so began his wanderlust, soon gaining himself a reputation as a playboy and socialite. Several relationships took place, with Alexandra's apparent acceptance. The Countess of Warwick asked him to build a train station near her house so that he may visit her more easily, and the prince was cited during divorce proceedings in 1869 having conducted an affair with the wife of a Member of Parliament while her husband was in the House of Commons.

Divorce was frowned upon; a man was able to file for divorce on the grounds of adultery but adultery alone was not considered enough of a reason for his wife to file for divorce. For a lady to have her name in the paper was acceptable only at birth, marriage and death, and in addition to these, for a man to be in it for anything other than business success risked society's rejection. For the prince to have his name in the paper for such irrefutable reasons lead to huge personal and public embarrassment.

While Edward remained devoted to his wife, their lives were increasingly separate. Edward was also known to frequent Parisian brothels where baths with seats were conveniently placed to assist in sex acts whilst filled with champagne![17] Edward's reputation as someone not born to reign was obviously apparent to his public through his all-embracing manner, through which they felt they knew him. From a child's viewpoint in *The Young Visiters:*

> It upsets me said the prince lapping up his strawberry ice all I want is peace and quiut [sic] and a little fun and here I am tied down to this life he said taking off his crown being royal has many painful drawbacks.[18]

In 1907 Elinor Gwyn published *Three Weeks*. The book was about a love affair between a nobleman and a Balkan princess.[19] The passionate tryst was so disapproved of that King Edward would not have the book mentioned in his presence. Boys at Eton found reading it would be punished. Edwardian Britain was somewhat a contradiction, with the appearance of beauty and morality, while some had a reputation for contravening this in every way. It was socially easier to have an affair to which most would turn a blind eye than to have your name in the divorce papers. Summarised by Kate Caffrey, the commandment which may be applied to the era is: 'Thou shalt not be found out'.[20]

The subsequent loosening of Victorian moral stricture came conveniently hand in hand with the wearing of the loose-fitting tea gown or tea dress. The upper and aristocratic classes were associated with partaking in extramarital affairs during this teatime interlude. There were no economic depressions during Edward VII's reign and it was a time of prosperity. Contraceptives had been introduced, and abortion had become a possibility so that fewer children were being born; as a result families were wealthier than they would have been otherwise. The Edwardian era came to be known as the Halcyon period, when such fripperies may be indulged in during a time of relative political peace, before the descent into the First World War.

Despatches – is he Mentioned? by Edgar Bundy (1862–1922), 1917. (Courtesy of James Harvey)

Princess Alexandra had an intense dislike for Germany which stemmed from the Prussian seizure of the Danish provinces of Schleswig and Holstein in the 1860s. Her emotions are telling in a letter she wrote to her son, George V, when he was made honorary colonel of a Prussian regiment in 1890:

> And so my Georgie boy has become a real live filthy blue-coated Pickelhaube German soldier!! Well, I never thought to have lived to see that! But never mind, it was your misfortune and not your fault.[21]

Edward VII possessed dynamic social aptitude which extended to bringing countries together, so British relations between some European countries strengthened, particularly France where he was known as 'Peacemaker'. The only country where relations did not benefit from Edward's charm was Germany, whose emperor was his nephew, Kaiser Wilhelm II.

Edward was widely accepting of all walks of life, making him a popular monarch whose influence helped reduce the social strictures of the Victorian era. However, there were limitations; for example he did not support the plight of the Suffragettes in their struggle for equality for women. However, his benevolence in the treatment of all nationalities and cultures as equals gained him a place in the hearts of many.

2

Will You Come to Tea?

An Edwardian hostess was expected to provide attractive premises, delicious food and drink, perfect service, and a handsome, well-dressed, agreeable company …
Kate Caffrey quoting Stella Gibbons, *The 1900s Lady,* 1976

Queen Victoria often entertained through teatime, introducing garden parties in 1865, and inviting wives and children of officers and soldiers to tea in Windsor Castle. While the queen would greet her guests and then leave them to enjoy tea, her daughters would remain, reputedly to make them feel at home.

Prince Edward and Princess Alexandra entertained in Marlborough House, where they lived until 1901 when Edward became king, at which time they moved to Buckingham Palace.[21] Marlborough House was known as a place of intimate tea parties where guests would be entertained during the London season from February until July. Princess Alexandra would invite her close friends and family to the Red Saloon, written about in *Lady's Realm*, a magazine for British women, as one of the most beautiful apartments in Marlborough House. Having spent his reign entertaining in Buckingham Palace, after the king's death Princess Alexandra reinstated the Red Saloon as a place where she had afternoon tea and in so doing rearranged the reception room in order to suit the habit. Sketches done by the royal family were placed on a table near the fire place for her guests to view.

Tea guests would arrive a few minutes before four o'clock when Princess Alexandra would enter the room with Miss Knollys, her Lady of the Bedchamber, a title given to the lady in attendance of the queen. The guests would rise at the entrance of the Queen and would then each be greeted with a handshake.

Ladies would entertain with tea parties in an era when the vast majority did not, and were not expected to, work. The etiquette involved at teatime was as formal a procedure as Princess Alexandra's, though without the pomp and ceremony of the hostess making an entrance. While procedure was formal, because teatime happened every day, family members would be involved in the serving process, following a formula which had become second nature.

Tea was always served by the host/hostess or a friend, never by a servant. Tea was never poured out, then passed several cups at a time, the way coffee may be, because it cools very quickly. Instead, it was always taken by the guest directly from the hands of the pourer.[22]

The guest may have brought their own servant with them. If not, a footman or housemaid would unpack the clothes of the guest, light the fire in the bedroom, and have hot water ready in their room, as well as putting out their dressing gown, shoes, and dress for dinner. Not until tea had finished should the guest be shown to their room by a servant. It was quite normal for 'At Homes' to take place in several houses of friends so that at least two or three visits may take up the afternoon. An alternative to the carriage, a motorised omnibus, was first seen in 1898, but not generally taken by ladies.

Visits, particularly to the country, often involved spending a night, when horse and carriage were the mode of transport. The horses and coachmen (there would often be two coachmen where the journey was long) would need rest before the return journey. Not until the introduction of the motorcar in the early 1900s were more spontaneous visits possible, bringing about change for those who could afford it.

The motorcar gradually became more common after the Edwardian era. Without it, visits were planned some time in advance. It was important that a guest should be made aware of whether or not he or she would be collected from the station by horse and carriage, or whether a taxi carriage should be hired. Dorothy Peel advises:

> to avoid misunderstanding it is better to make the point clear. For instance, if the hostess wrote, 'I am sorry that we cannot send to meet you, but you will find cabs at the station,' the guest would certainly pay for the cab but if the hostess worded her letter somewhat in this fashion, 'We should have sent to meet you, but unfortunately, the horses have to go in the opposite direction; I have, however, engaged a cab, so you need have no further bother about the matter', it would be evident that the host considered the cab hire his affair.[23]

On the arrival of a guest, the servant should have been informed how the transport was to be paid for. Money would be given to the servant if the hostess was to pay for their guest's transport. This practice was not common in London, where the guest was expected to pay for their own transport.

By the Edwardian period, tea had become a significant social event. Invitees may be carefully selected, not only to socialise with, but to show off finery, appearance being all. Letters and invitations would be written on cream paper and sealed with wax, partly to stop prying eyes.

So important was how tea was served, that Dorothy Peel wrote that it is 'astonishing to find how ignorant some servants are on such points, even though they have come from good houses and describe themselves as experienced'.[24]

Before four o'clock women would drive from house to house, leaving calling cards as they did so. Calling cards were introduced as the social circle had widened to include 'the upper ten thousand'. This produced a snobbery of where exactly those visiting for tea or otherwise were from. Calling cards were to be left at a house if the person visited was not home. That person would decide whether or not she wished to return the call and in so doing would assess the suitability of the person who had left the card. If their social reputation and standing as well as financial position were acceptable then the call may be returned, enabling the visited to decide whether or not the visitee was socially within their realm!

> From four o'clock, before which hour cards and notes had been left (for this was a card-leaving period and the telephone was a novelty), until six-thirty women drove from house to house to find each crowded with women and elderly men who drank tea, iced coffee, or cup, or ate sandwiches, cakes, strawberries and cream, and ices, listened to professional musicians, and gossiped. Tea-visiting over, the lady of fashion would perhaps take a turn in the Park and a short rest before dressing for dinner in a gown cut well off the shoulders and, although short sleeved, never actually sleeveless.[26]

Arriving for tea. (Author's family album)

Boating on the Thames on a dreamy afternoon was a standard part of Edwardian courtship.
Drawing entitled 'Dolce far niente' by W. Hatherell. (*The Mansell Collection*)

When visitors departed, the servant would open the door for the guest and also the door of the carriage, tucking the rug around the guest before instructing the coachman or cabman on where to go; 'In many houses the servants are ill-trained, and make no attempt to help the visitor into her carriage or cab.'[27]

Providing they had been introduced in the correct manner at an 'At Home', a lady would be allowed to meet a gentleman outside of the home in a tea room or at a *Thé Dansant* (tea dance) to play tennis or perhaps punt on the river. Restaurants deemed suitable for young ladies may also be a place to meet a suitor or gentleman friend.

Ladies were not expected to take part in the serving of breakfast, lunch or dinner, but tea was the exception, the expectation being that once it had been brought into the drawing room, it should be served by the mistress of the house.

Tea would be served in a fine tea set for acquaintances, less fine for close friends and family:

'Oh Marilla, can I use the rosebud spray tea set?'
'No, indeed! The rosebud tea set! Well, what next? You know I never use that except for the minister or the Aids. You'll put down the old brown tea set.'[28]

It was not uncommon for ladies to go without in order to be seen to provide for one's guests. Later in the Edwardian era Dorothy Peel suggests that to serve tea in an earthenware pot was acceptable, though further investigation suggests this view was not held by most, as seen in *Anne of Green Gables*:

Mrs. Rachel … had taken a mental note of everything that was on that table. There were three plates laid, so that Marilla must be expecting some one home with Matthew to tea; but the dishes were everyday dishes and there was only crab-apple preserve and one kind of cake so that the expected company could not be any particular company.

What was served depended on the company. A fine blend of tea, or orange pekoe, would be served to lesser-known guests, while a lower blend of fannings or dust would be served to close friends. This form of service is reiterated in *How to Keep House*, 1906 in which newly married women are advised on what to expect of their servants, suggesting that champagne should be reserved for acquaintances and wine for friends.

Tea was used as a social forum during which liaisons may be conducted between potential beaus and acquaintances. *Howard's End* gives example of this, illustrated well in the verbiage, despite the interest shown not being one of romance when Margaret wishes to ask Leonard Bast to tea: '… while her lips talked culture, her heart was planning to invite him to tea.'

Tea parties allowed the blossoming of romance. Among games played was hide and seek, with ladies being 'too afraid' to hide alone, and pairings of young men and women scurrying into nooks and crannies of the house. As long as the pair did not take too long to be discovered, this provided single girls with at least a little covert behaviour.

Innocence was preserved so much so that, were a daughter not engaged to be married after one season, and certainly after two, it became less likely that she

would have been sheltered from the wiles of men. A story illustrating this is where
the mistress of the house was showing some innocent young ladies into the library,
only to find her daughter with a man on the floor in front of a roaring fire. Quickly
exiting the room, on being asked by one of the young ladies what they were doing,
she replied with, 'Mending the carpet – so kind.'[29]

   Children were preferred to be seen and not heard, having their tea in the nursery
between five and six o'clock, after which some joined their parents for pudding, or
their mother may sit with them and have a cup of tea.[30]

   The lucky few however, were invited to tea parties for children by the very few
who gave them. One family gave children's parties at certain hours according to
their ages, with the younger ones invited from three until six o'clock, the older from
six until eight and the teenagers from eight until ten. Carriages would come and go,
delivering and collecting, though there were some parents who thought that such a
party at a young age was too much excitement and so forbade the invitation.

   Life for children generally took place in the nursery with interludes of walks and
occasional visits to the drawing room. Some houses would have a miniature table
and chairs to accommodate the children. One story is of a grandfather who, when
discovering that his granddaughter had been put in the corner as punishment for a
misdeed, painted garden scenes on the walls of that corner, naturally assuming that
this would not be her last transgression.

His First Birthday by Frederick Morgan (1856–1927). (Courtesy of James Harvey)

3

How to Dress for Tea

A large fraction of our time was spent in changing our clothes, particularly in winter when you came down to breakfast ready for church in your 'best dress' made probably of velvet ... After church you went into tweeds. You always changed again before tea into a tea gown ... however small your allowance a different dinner dress for each night was considered necessary.

Lady Cynthia Asquith, *Remember and Be Glad*, 1952

Afternoon tea around four o'clock conjures up images of polite, beautifully dressed ladies chit-chatting over cups of steaming tea with delicate cakes and breads. Gloves were often worn by these ladies, and in accordance with this it was considered polite for biscuits to be provided which would be easier to eat with gloves on than sandwiches, the fillings of which may mark the gloves. If the mistress of the house had warm hands, she would most likely wear gloves for greeting guests where there were more than just one or two of them.[31] Tea's social interlude was accompanied by a full change of clothing into the tea dress, aimed to assist in its relaxation. It soon became the rage, with magazines containing pictures of continually progressive styles as the era advanced.

The Edwardian era showed clear class divisions. The middle classes were deemed morally astute while the aristocracy and upper classes were seen as hedonistic in their privilege and use of time, ladies changing as many as five times a day. This saw its historical influence in Louis XIV and then Napoleon III who found it the 'utmost displeasure' were the same dress worn in his presence.[32]

The diurnal and nocturnal time of aristocratic and high-bourgeois society was divided into pretexts, marked by a relentless tempo for dressing and undressing; and doing so appropriately involved a veritable gnosis ... [Etiquette books provide a] reference point of temporal and spatial oppositions (night/day, morning/evening, winter/summer, interior/exterior; town/country) that constituted basic dichotomies within which an impressive armory of vestimentary opportunities could unfurl: the wardrobe.[33]

Touring

From Mlle Louise Piret, rue
Richer. 1. Suit with fitted jacket.
2. Travel outfit with jacket.
3. Travel dress with bolero.
4. Dress trimmed with bands of
stitching and cape. 5. Travel hat
from Magasins du Louvre.

From Aymé et Cie., boul. de la
Madeleine. 1. Batiste toilette.
2. Dress with pleated bodice and
corselet. 3. Organdy dress.
4. Toilette in printed foulard.
5. Toilette with unmatched bodice.
6. Elegant chapeau from Magasins
du Louvre.

At the
Racetrack

Above and below: Women's fashion adverts in
La Mode Illustrée. (Author's collection)

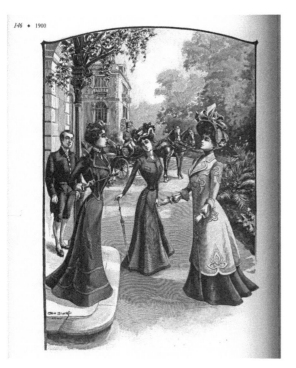

Thanks to an Englishman, Charles
Worth, sewing patterns were
introduced in the 1850s. This eased
the burden of having to own several
dresses in order to look the part.

After 'luncheon' a lady would
go out on her calls which would
involve visiting town for leisurely
errands, or simply going for a walk.
From around three o'clock her maid
would be summoned to help her
into her tea dress. The tea dress, tea
gown, 'teagie' or 'robe d'interieur'
was styled on the dressing gown,
its natural relation, being worn
indoors at a time when comfort
was paramount. Lady Randolph
Churchill was seen as daring in her
taking this comfort to a new level by
wearing a kimono.

Day dress outside of teatime
involved an all in one undergarment,

corset and coutil, with boning, stays and silk pads for the waist and under arms put in place so as to create a shapely silhouette which became known as the S-shape.

Corsets were the least comfortable part of everyday dress, the desired waist measurement being an impossible eighteen inches. Thanks to a combination of the Rational Dress Society of 1881, the introduction of compulsory education for women, and their demand for greater freedom, not wearing a corset became gradually acceptable. The removal of the corset for at least a period of the day while wearing the tea dress, provided longed for relief.

Among the negative health issues associated by the Victorians with the corset were that they caused gallstones, though still today women are more likely to suffer from gallstones than men. Constricting the full expansion of the lungs led to lack of oxygen to the blood, the prime reason for discomfort.[34]

A petticoat would be laid on the floor before the dress was buttoned, not forgetting that stockings held up with garters or suspenders attached to the corset also formed part of underwear.

A panel was discreetly placed in the undergarments, whether an all-in-one or frilly knickers and camisole, so that when nature called, clothes removal was not too timely a process. Blouses were popular in the Edwardian era, with a stiff belt-like material between it and a skirt, securely attached.

A hat adorned with feathers, flowers and even a stuffed bird, was

Women's fashion adverts (*Above:* Author's collection *Below: La Mode Illustree*)

Above: Women's fashion adverts in *La Mode Illustrée*. (Author's collection)
Below: Woman in mourning. (Author's collection)

worn when out of the house. It would often be secured with hat pins, only adding to the long-winded dressing process. Gloves with buttons were worn outside of the house, and boots also with buttons. All in all, dressing for ladies, until the First World War, was a time consuming process.

Queen Victoria wore black for forty years following the death of Prince Albert, until her own death in 1901. Widows were expected to mourn for their husbands for two and a half years. The first year and a day were spent fully clothed in black crepe. Following this, it was acceptable to introduce more fanciful material such as velvet and lace which may be used for the second year. For the following final six months, colours such as grey, mauve and violet may be used for clothing before mourning would cease.

The most popular material was black crepe, or crape, as it was referred to in mourning, differentiating it from standard crepe. White crape was used for the bonnets of widows. The mourning time frame meant that by the end of the mourning period, fashions may have changed. All clothes were made or bought in black. When Prince Albert died, to show respect to the queen, stationery was edged in black. People tied black or purple ribbon around scent bottles, and some children even wore dark ribbon around their arms.

Sunshine was avoided as the fashion was to have as white a face as possible. Effects of the Industrial Revolution lead to chemical additions within make up. Despite misleading names such as Blanc d'Argent and Bland de Perles, they contained unappetising ingredients such as arsenic or prussic acid. Cecil Beaton described his Aunt Jessie's application of the whitening paint as 'whitewash'.

Later in the Edwardian era it became fashionable to show you had been abroad, holidaying in the South of France or Italy, and so a tan was not such a bad thing. Fashionably white faces truly came to an end after the First World War and with Coco Chanel's introduction of tanned skin in 1920.[35]

The Victorian and Edwardian era frowned upon ladies powdering their noses, 'if they shone, they shone'.[36] Instead, what may be got away with was using Papier Poudre, a

Later in the Edwardian period, fashions had become more relaxed. (Author's collection)

thin leaf of paper which, when applied to the nose, effectively left a near matt result. It was fashionable to wear rouge. Lips and cheeks may be tattooed with a natural rose, and one book even suggests lighting a pin in a flame and placing it on the eye lids so as to act as eye liner. While this recipe did come originally from advice in Roman times, it re-emerged hundreds of years later![37] Some ladies 'brightened their sparkle' with the lethal plant, belladonna, better known as deadly nightshade. Cosmetics were not easily obtainable commercially until Gordon Selfridge supplied them in 1909, by which time ingredients and their harm were beginning to be realised. A vivid picture of an Edwardian lady's dress and make up is visualised by a young writer:

> She looked very beautiful with some red roses in her hat and the dainty red ruge in
> her cheeks looked quite the thing.[38]

Late nineteenth century vanity also included nipple piercing, considered to improve the shape of the bust as well as to provide a pleasing sensation between nipple and material! This fashion had mostly faded by the Edwardian era.[39]

Lavender, rose and violet were popular fragrances. With deodorants not becoming widely available until later in the century, less understandable is 'eau de corsage' which was the faint smell of sweat, said to be attractive to gentlemen.

Light-brown hair was the desired colour, those with blonde hair being considered unfortunate, partly because the fashionable colours of the era were rose, pink and mauve, thought to suit brown hair. It was curled with tongs until a chemical process using rollers was developed.

Aged eighteen, if a young lady was to wear her hair up, it would indicate that she was open to romantic offers. Outside of the bedroom, her hair remained up for the rest of her life. In contrast to the costume jewellery of their elders, young Edwardian ladies wore little jewellery, possibly just a simple string of pearls.

Edwardian ladies were educated in how to laugh and not to shriek. Low voices were considered ladylike, and giggling as opposed to hearty laughter. Certain words should be pronounced in certain ways, such as 'blouse' should be pronounced 'blooze' and 'lahndry' for 'laundry'. The final 'g' in words such as 'hunting' and 'shooting' was dropped by ladies who considered themselves country girls, a habit adopted first by their brothers.[40]

Prince Edward's social whirl allowed an interest in fashion which was regarded as suited to the era and its change. He introduced the wearing of a black tie with a dinner jacket, where previously it had been more common to wear a white tie with tails. He wore a smoking jacket for teatime, and introduced trousers with side creases as opposed to back and front creases common today. His influence also lead to Norfolk jackets, originally worn for sport, being seen as everyday wear.

As king, Edward's reputation as a setter of fashions and impeccable dress sense does not go hand in hand with the story of Sonia, the daughter of Alice Keppell, one of King Edward's favoured ladies, of a game she played with 'Kingy'. When he came to tea she would place a piece of thickly buttered bread, butter side down, on each of his trouser legs. They would each place a small bet on which piece of butter-slathered bread would reach the floor first![41]

Men, often with a curled moustache, would change for tea out of whatever they had been wearing, probably shooting clothes or tweeds, and put on a smoking jacket which had the feeling of sumptuous abandon associated with the looseness of the tea dress. Day dress of 'black morning coat, dark grey striped trousers, and a black waistcoat, with a white pique slip in it, and black boots – is de rigueur. Many men wear light spats, and there is no harm in a button-hole.'[42]

Not only did the mistress and master of the house dress for tea, whether in the boudoir, the drawing room or at a tea dance, but the occasion necessitated that the uniform worn by the maid serving tea must be neat, tidy and clean. Service would involve a

Men's fashion adverts in *La Mode Illustrée*. (Author's collection)

change of apron and the wearing of a cap and shoes with soft soles, so that her entrance into the drawing room would be a peaceful one, without the possible clatter of hard soles on the floor.

By the Edwardian era the teatime ritual had extended into wider circles with its being moved from boudoir to drawing room, (though for intimate teatimes, the boudoir may still be used), and tea dances or gardens. The tea dress became a little more elaborate and took a risqué form of 'le fif-o'-clock' or 'cinq a sept'. This came from Paris, where the hour of tea was associated with a time during which a lady may be visited for 'tea' by her lover. It was understood that this hour was one during which she would not be disturbed by anyone, even her husband, who was probably making his own such liaison at the time!

While affairs may be accepted and not spoken of, were they to be leaked, there was little forgiveness, aptly put by Mrs Pat Campbell, who said that what was done in the bedroom was 'immaterial … as long as one did not do it in the street and frighten the horses.'[43] A severe example is seen in the reaction of Lord Londonderry. His wife conducted an affair with Mr Cust, whose love of the ladies preceded him. During their liaison, the impassioned letters Lady Londonderry wrote were kept by Mr Cust. The Marchioness of Ripon, who later took the place of Lady Londonderry in Mr Custs's affection, found these letters. Not only did

The Edwardian Tea Taster

I don't suppose it's the sort of thing I'll find
  on the Portobello Road, if indeed its like
  was ever made: this perfect Edwardian gent
  in a frock coat and puce velveteen trousers,
  with a minuscule real cane, top hat, silks;
the whole design complete down to brass and pewter
  fitments, and fiddly gas ducts – now cut off,
  for it seems the device has been electrified.
  And it works! As I discover when I tip
  some used leaves ineptly in its warming jug
  and thereby set in motion an arm that lifts
  a tepid spoonful to the taster's lips
  – at which he bends double, sputters, spits:
generating all around (and from above) a chorus
  of deep laughter: a moist, throaty utterance
  I can't, for several seconds, get a hold of,
then wake with it bubbling from my lips, the sound
  already dispersed; and now verifiable
  only by an odd, and oddly intimate,
  disarrangement of the muscles of my face
  – that, and a willingness, hours early, to get up;
  to make tea the way our Grandmas did:
  a patient, hot viscous infusion, then served
(why thank you, little man) very nearly black.

Maurice Riordan, Irish Poet

she read them to her friends, but sent them to Lord Londonderry. Never again did he speak to his wife, not even from his deathbed. The Marchioness of Ripon sent a telegram in apology thirty years later, following the death of Lord Londonderry; perhaps needless to say, she was not forgiven.

The role of the tea dress was criticised by *The Times* as having digressed into one of beauty, perhaps designed to tantalise: 'Of course it in no way represents the dressing gown of utility… It is absolutely useless, and utterly ridiculous … to all intents and purposes a *desabille*.' To anger the writer further, the tea dress was seen as extravagant with its only being worn once or twice before a new dress was thought necessary by fashionable ladies.44 With suggestive associations, ladies wearing tea dresses apparently formed the habit of conducting conversation and games which alluded to the dress worn. So while gossip was purveyed as the pleasure partaken by women at tea parties, for some, conversation was actually not at the forefront of their attention!

The tea dress was made of a light material such as chiffon or a light silk or satin. It tended to dip at the neck in a more seductive shape while the light material would reveal the natural curve of the waist. Lace was also added at times, and in the latter part of the Edwardian era, a shrug or long cardigan or tunic-like garment usually made of lightly transparent material was added. The Art Nouveau movement from 1890 to 1910 meant that adding patterns such as flowers to a dress became an essential part of keeping up with the latest trends. Despite the tea dress gaining a reputation as risqué, having several of them to choose from was considered a vital part of a lady's wardrobe.

The Waltz and the Two-Step were essentially the only two dances in the 1870s. The desire for something new and exciting saw the influence of ragtime music and dance from America, sometimes seen via Paris from 1895 until 1918. These dances were associated with the lower classes and so initially would not be danced by the upper classes, though calmed versions were gradually introduced to tea dances. The One-Step became extremely popular partly due to the simplicity of its movement, and the Hesitation Waltz was a more graceful form of dance considered respectable by all.

In 1910 the tango was introduced via a play, *The Sunshine Girl*, in which the Argentinian dance was seen at the Gaiety Theatre. It was considered so risqué that the Kaiser banned his daughter-in-law from taking lessons. The *Dancing Times,* a magazine in circulation at the time, contains an article describing a tempered version of its Latin counterpart of gyrating hips and dramatic movement:

> The original tango may have been voluptuous and risque and changed the modest dance platform seen so far. That does not prevent the present edition of it being decorous, refined and graceful. … The Tango is graceful, decorous and worthy of a place in any ballroom. If you doubt me, go to one of the 'Thés Dansants' organized by the Boston Club on Wednesday afternoons at The Waldorf Hotel, and you will be Charmed.

The tango became a craze, with newspapers reporting, 'Tango, Tango, Tango!' Large venues such as Earls Court and the Palais de Dance began to host events which soon became available to the masses.45 Tickets could be bought on the door of venues hosting the dances, paying a little extra if you wished to dance, rather than simply sip tea. Mothers were reluctant to allow their daughters to take part in the tango, even within the relative safety of private homes where dances also took place:

> I am one of the many matrons upon whom devolves the task of guiding a girl through the mazes of a London season, and I am face to face with a state of affairs in most, but not all, of the ballrooms calling for the immediate attention of those in like case. My grandmother has often told me of the shock she experienced on first beholding the polka, but I wonder what she would have said had she been asked to introduce a well-brought-up girl to the scandalous travesties of dancing which are, for the first time in my recollection, bringing more young men to parties than are needed ... I ask hostesses to let one know what houses to avoid by indicating in some way on their invitation cards whether the 'Turkey Trot,' the 'Boston' (the beginner of the evil,) and the 'Tango' will be permitted.[46]

The anxiety the tango brought to some meant that invitations sent for tea dances indicated which dances were to take place. However, others embraced these tea dances, the Duchesses of Marlborough and Manchester among those considered 'chief tango hostesses'.

Thés Dansants meant that social lives became far less restricted, *The Times* reporting in May 1913, 'What a happy innovation on such an afternoon would be the "tea-dance"! Men usually fight shy of the ladies' tea-hour, but few of them can resist the pleasure of a waltz or a Boston; so try the tea-dance idea ...!'[47] Tea dances that took place in theatres involved watching hired dancers go through their steps while

THE HAREM GIRL.

Above left: Dancing couple. (Courtesy of Richard Powers, dance historian at Stanford University)
Above right: Advert for Harem pants (Author's collection)
Opposite: Elaborate tea dresses. (Courtesy of Richard Powers)

the onlookers were served tea and indulged in accompanying dainties. Following the dance performance in theatres would be a fashion show of the latest ensembles.

The Regency period influenced Edwardian fashion so that dresses no longer had large skirts and severely corseted waists. In 1909 a Parisian fashion designer, Paul Poiret, introduced fashions that were inspired by the Orient and Paris's *Ballets Russes*, the twentieth century's most influential ballet company. Poiret designed a hobble skirt and, while not worn with a corset, restricted movement, hence its name. Poiret also introduced tunics which draped over the skirt.

Women were unable to take a full step wearing this skirt and so some had pleats or slits discreetly put into them so that they would at least be able to move more comfortably. This may be seen as symbolic of the freedoms pioneered by the Suffragette movement. With one hand women had been freed of the strictures of the corset, but with the other, Poiret's hobble skirt reminded them of their political and social restriction. He is quoted as saying 'I freed the bosom, shackled the legs'.[48] The inability to dance in these skirts meant they were very unpopular and led to their speedy demise. Poiret then designed Harem trousers, based on styles worn by sultans and seen in Middle Eastern harems, which only a few daring women wore.

Above and below: Dancing steps and shoes. (Courtesy of Richard Powers, dance historian at Stanford University)

Designers and dressmakers fashioned clothes around stockings, waists and shoes suited to dancing the tango. Hats were always worn outside of the home, and the tango hat was designed when dancing took place at Thés Dansants in tea gardens.

The motorcar was embraced by some Miss Dorothy Levitt's 1908 work *The Woman in the Car* advised women to avoid 'lace or fluffy adjuncts to your toilette'. Both the tea dress and the car played a part in helping forge the road to women's liberation. By 1912 changing several times each day was no longer as common, with *La Mode Illustrée*, a magazine focused on fashion since the 1860s, writing of *tout-aller* costumes which could be worn all day until dinner, when a lady would transform from a caterpillar by day [to a] butterfly by night. Nothing could be more comfortable than a caterpillar and nothing more made for love than a butterfly. There must be dresses that crawl and dresses that fly. The butterfly does not go to market, and the caterpillar does not go to a ball.[49]

By 1913, *La Mode Illustrée* was writing of the motorcar and the 'unknown corners of which we would always have remained in ignorance without our blessed automobiles'.[50] Comfort in fashion was the focus with Chanel stepping in with unencumbered fashions further freeing women of the vogues dictated by society.

The end of the Edwardian era saw the foxtrot, a dance which combined both slow and quick steps of the dances before it, culminating the dances of an era which was about to come to an end with the onset of the First World War in 1914.[51]

Opposite: Dancing couples. Note the inner skirt behind the split. (Courtesy of Richard Powers, dance historian at Stanford University)
Below: Dancing the tango. (Courtesy of Richard Powers, dance historian at Stanford University)

THE TANGO

THE TANGO

4

From Tea Houses to Thés Dansants

Tea at a Renaissance villa? Nothing had been said about it yet. But if it did come to that – how Lucy would enjoy it!

E. M. Forster, *A Room with a View*, 1908

Three-tiered stands laden with sandwiches, cakes, hot crumpets and sometimes bonbons, alongside pretty teapots and china cups filled with tea or coffee, evoke memories for those whose grannies or great-grannies were accustomed to tea ceremony. Such temptation is the finale of what began as a warming drink. Hong Kong, Pakistan, China and Japan are among countries with their own tea ceremonies dating back to way before tea gained in significance in Britain in the nineteenth century. Britain's influence spread to its once colonial countries in East Africa, Australia and New Zealand, so that tea in one form or another is a worldwide pleasure.

When asked what people think of when describing the British, tea has become an institution with which we are unquestionably linked. 200 years before afternoon tea became a daily ritual, coffee shops and tea houses were set up as places where men may meet, reputed to be noisy smoke-filled dens, the only women seen in them being those who were serving, or those of ill repute. It was not until later in the nineteenth century that it was considered acceptable for respectable women to visit them, when they became civilised houses of hospitality. Such forums of conversation are thought to have seen the birth of the suffrage movement.

England's first coffee shop opened in Oxford in 1652, where the Grand Café now stands. There followed Greek coffee shops and later, more English coffee houses. These places of discussion over coffee saw the humble beginnings of business enterprise, nicknamed 'penny universities', a penny having to be paid upon entrance. Among them is Lloyds of London on Tower Street which began with marine insurance being the hot topic of conversation. It grew in reputation and is now an international insurance company. The London Stock Exchange and the auction houses of Sotheby's and Christie's had similar beginnings.[52] Ironically, Lloyds of London ended up insuring the ships of both legal and smuggled imports of tea. In addition to hives of business, social chit-chat naturally took place. Not long after their arrival, coffee houses were strongly disapproved of by Charles II who feared scandalous rumours about his reign and his Ministers.[53]

Tea served in coffee and tea houses was brewed early in the morning due to the need to measure it for tax purposes. This taxation was prohibitive to tea's enjoyment, as well as coffee and hot chocolate, causing 'no small prejudice to the liquor and inconvenience to the Drinker, for the Excise officer was to survey it before any could be sold, and was not to survey it above once or twice daily.'[54]

Tax had to be paid from 1660 until 1689 according to the drink's measurement in liquid form. This meant that what would be served as the day progressed was a strong brew which would not have tasted like the more delicate tea enjoyed after 1689, when it was taxed according to the weight of the leaf rather than liquid.[55] Tea could then be bought and taken home by men who had conducted business in tea and coffee houses or by a servant who had been tasked with the errand.

Green and black tea imported from China, as well as Turkish coffee, was sold in coffee houses while business was being conducted. Tea's popularity and profit margin lead to its being adulterated by some sellers with sheep's dung. This was relatively harmless compared with green tea in the eighteenth and early nineteenth centuries which, when not the genuine article, had copper carbonate and lead chromate added. One tea dealer saw green tea as a 'secret assassin'. Partly because of this fear, black tea became more popular.[56] With England's interest in tea from Ceylon and India, in came unadulterated tea and the demise of green tea and its associated risk.

In the early nineteenth century alcohol was drunk by all, including children to a lesser extent; adding a little alcohol to a glass of water helping negate contamination. Thankfully, the Band of Hope, a Christian charity in Leeds educating children on drug and alcohol abstinence, successfully fought that children should not consume any alcohol at all, its members pledging their support in the mid-1800s. Due to its cost, English Poor Law policy limited the drinking of tea by children, so that it accompanied supper on Sundays only.

Outside of coffee shops, business discussion was frequently accompanied by alcohol whether in an Inn, Public House or private home. The realisation that business was more successfully conducted without the possibility of alcohol fuelling the discussion influenced the Temperance movements, which started in Scotland and Ireland in the 1820s. The upper classes supported temperance movements, concerned that alcohol consumption among the working classes may affect the quality of their work. This resulted in the signing of documents pledging lifelong temperance by many.

Further Temperance associations were set up both among religious and political parties. However, in England, any legal suggestion of prohibition was met with vehement disregard, illustrating the British attitude to alcohol – never would they accept its prohibition. Servants in the Edwardian era were given a supply of ale throughout their working day. There were some, however, who set an example, one being Sir Walter Trevelyan of Wallington Hall in Northumberland who became known as the Apostle of Temperance. All wine and spirits were locked away, to be donated to scientific research on the death of Sir Walter.[57]

'Totally' drinking tea could possibly be the derivation of the word 'teetotal'.[58] As seen in the first chapter, there were still those who worried about the effects of tea, despite alcohol's blatant repercussions and tea being a preferable alternative. Coffee and tea shops continued to be opened where business discussion may take place, unhindered by alcohol's influence.

By the Edwardian era tea had been enjoyed by many for such a long time that most recognised its benefits as soothing. There were some, however, who still doubted its suitability for all. The distinct few saw it as harmful to their servants for ridiculous reasons such as that it should be reserved for the upper classes and aristocracy because it may get in the way of the work of servants. One should imagine these poor victims of their employer's misapprehension looked longingly at the tea served to their master and mistress while sneaking in an unseen sip below stairs!

Invitations to tea were sent out on 'At Home' cards from a week to three weeks before the event. Teas would be carefully organised events which, because they happened most days with or without family, were a natural part of every day and until tea dances took place later in the nineteenth century, were simple affairs, though with a strictly followed etiquette. Printed on the top corner of the 'At Home' card would be 'garden party', 'tennis', 'croquet', or whichever game might be played, with the hostess's name underneath and the date. All ages may be invited and so entertainment ranged from Punch and Judy to listening to a band, often commandeered from a local regiment. Unless dancing were to take place, usually under the stars or in a tent, these parties tended to end around seven o'clock.

In books on etiquette, such as one written by Marie Byard in 1884, advice was given on how to arrange your drawing room for a tea dance:

> The back dining room, or study, is generally arranged as a tearoom, for the guests to enter on arriving, and in small houses the ladies will also leave their cloaks there. A table must be arranged on one side, with a table cloth, cups, and saucers, tea and coffee, cut bread and butter, and cakes, and a maid must be stationed behind this to attend, while another maid assists the ladies to take off their wraps.

For a young lady to leave the house without a chaperone was unacceptable. Men were not trusted not to take advantage. It was assumed that, given the chance, with just a few minutes alone in a drawing room during tea, he would take his chance. So as to avoid this possible slur on a young lady's reputation that 'Cecilia has got into a scrape', prior to marriage chaperones were deemed essential; young ladies' innocence was childlike, so coveted was their youth. Everything they did from taking a bath and having breakfast to being escorted home from a ball was done under the watchful eye of a servant or chaperone. Many really had little to no introduction in what to expect of a husband once married.

With ladies not frequenting public houses or inns, the arrival of tea rooms and coffee shops with tea dances saw the loosening of this social sanctuary. Possibly influenced by French Colonial Morocco, where maidens danced while their elders drank tea, tea dances took place in private homes and some larger well-established hotels, department stores and restaurants. The Aerated Bread Company opened the first public tea room where people could meet instead of at a public house. Many more were opened to the extent that a booklet containing the locations of all of ABC's tea rooms in London was published. Joseph Lyons soon followed suit, opening a tea shop in Piccadilly in 1894 which was the second of its kind, with a band, tea and plenty of space for dancing. It slowly became more widely accepted that ladies may go out to tea without a chaperone, though usually accompanied by at least a friend or two. More Lyon's tea rooms were opened so that it was not long before men and women met regularly at these tea-fuelled establishments, which also saw the beginnings of families eating out.

During and before the Edwardian era, great opulent buildings sprang up, their contents associated with the increasing privilege of the time. Among them were the Ritz, the Piccadilly Hotel, and Selfridge's. While these venues tended to be for the upper echelons of society, dancing took place in theatres and village halls or

Tea at Gunter's from 'An Edwardian Season', by John Strickland (1908–1996). (Courtesy of James Harvey)

wherever the desire took people, so that it was not long before dancing at teatime was enjoyed by all. An orchestra, sometimes referred to as a 'palm court orchestra' would play while the afternoon was danced away. No longer did the young have to wait for an invitation in order to socialise.

The social events of tea also lead to tea gardens, most likely a copy of the Dutch 'tavern garden teas'. The upper classes and aristocracy would meet in these gardens, such as the Hurlingham Club in London, where they would be served tea alongside entertainment such as concerts, beautiful garden walks, bowling, and perhaps even gambling. On each table at these tea gardens would be placed a small wooden box labelled T.I.P.S., which stood for To Insure Prompt Service.

Tea at home in the garden is documented as a clear and happy memory by Miss Ponsonby:

> they hold parasols, they sit in basket-chairs with cushions covered in jap silk, grouped round a table. The table has a white embroidered cloth on it, and a silver tea-tray loaded with silver tea-things that include a strange object like a hunting-horn, which extinguishes the flame under the kettle. Flowered china plates hold thin bread-and-butter, cucumber sandwiches, hot scones, seed-cake and sugar-cakes and home-made biscuits, and there is iced coffee as well as tea to drink. The ladies lean forward so that their hats cluster together like a huge bouquet above the table as the gossip becomes more exciting.[59]

5

Expectations of a Mistress

As people advance in life they are inclined to think much of a cup of tea or coffee, and rightfully are very particular as to the manner in which these are prepared.

Janet McKenzie Hill, *A Guide for Edwardian Servants*, 1908

'Lady' was applied to a woman of the upper classes or aristocracy. It was reserved only for them, so that anyone outside that social domain would not be referred to as a lady, despite the fact that social standing is not indicative of behaviour associated with being called a lady! A lady was 'a woman in easy circumstances, assured, socially so well placed that everywhere she would be accorded respectful consideration: one who could not possibly accept paid employment nor would need to; one whose father, brothers and husband were landowners, perhaps Members of Parliament or safe in the upper echelons of the Law, the Army, or the Church.'[60] Ladies were not expected to show their feelings openly, which may part explain the British reputation for formality and reserve. To show one's feelings was considered 'servants behaviour'. The warmth of Queen Alexandra was in marked contrast to what was considered to represent the Edwardian lady, her showing warmth and compassion with a lively and enthusiastic nature.[61]

Before the days of modern appliances, the running of a household was a full time job. To give an example of the labour involved, every morning a housemaid would scatter damp tea leaves over the carpet which would collect dust, before being swept up. Though a *lady* was not generally known to play a part in this, she would be expected to know enough about the running of her household so that she may guide her servants in what was expected of them. An example is the Keppels, who mixed with aristocracy, some being their relations. In their house in Grosvenor Street, they had a butler, a cook-housekeeper, three maids, a boot-boy, a nanny and later a governess. Employing a butler was more costly than a manservant and therefore showed those who may visit how wealthy the family might be, appearance in Edwardian times being everything to many. It was not unheard of for a lady to go without, eating buns and such like instead of more varied and expensive fare, so that she may afford to employ a butler and welcome guests to tea in the manner in which she wished to be perceived.

Until 1765 when Queen Charlotte commissioned Josiah Wedgewood to make a teapot of earthenware, tea was served in a silver pot. With her patronage, the earthenware tea set changed this silver façade, only afforded by the wealthy. It was named *Queensware* and was quickly copied in Europe so that tea drinking was extended to those whose pockets may not quite reach to the excesses of silver. Mr Bumble in Oliver Twist is seen inspecting the authenticity of the pot of the matron of the workhouse!

Teatime etiquette started with answering the door. If done by a maid, she should always have a clean apron on standby, regardless of what kind of domestic work was being undertaken when the guest arrived. She would wear a large apron or slip over her black dress and muslin apron, specifically so that when answering the door for tea, her dress would remain clean. When answered by a footman or a butler, 'even in large houses the footman is sometimes seen struggling into his coat as he traverses the hall.'[62] Answering the door was not as simple as it sounds. Servants were instructed to open it wide, never peer around it, and to speak clearly, taking note of the name of the visitor. Servants answering the door were instructed on what should be said, answering 'Yes, sir', or 'madam'; or, in the event of no-one being at home, simply saying 'not at home'.[63] The mistress of a larger house would tell the servant in which room she would like to receive her guests. The footman, called by his first name, or the butler, called by his surname by his employer and Mr So-and-so by servants, ushered the visitors in to the presence of the mistress of the house. The footman would open the door, the butler in the absence of a footman. With no footman or butler, these tasks fell to the housemaid who would both answer the door and bring tea into the drawing room.

Having taken the visitor's coat, the servant would pause at the door of the room where the introduction was to take place. The servant may then open the door, stand aside for the entrance of the guest, and announce their name. The door should then be shut, at which point the servant should make him or herself scarce, but within hearing distance so that when the hostess rang the bell for attention, she may be in quick attendance. Calling a maid may be done in a variety of ways. One lady recalls her aunt calling her maid by blowing into a speaking tube! The more usual way would have been to summon a servant via a bell which would ring in the kitchen.

Gentlemen were expected to make tea visits and were judged fashionable if gloves, coat, silk hat and umbrella or stick were not removed and given to a servant, but instead laid aside in the drawing room, so as to look as if just passing by. 'Young men paid their duty calls at Sunday teas and sowed the seed of further invitations.'[64]

Fires were often lit during a tea visit, another duty which fell to the servant. This would only be unnecessary if tea took place in a morning-room or 'boudoir'.

While ensuring that tea and bouillon were kept hot, the servant in attendance was also responsible for ensuring that pikelets, tea cakes or crumpets were hot. The task of pouring the tea was reserved for the mistress of the house. Princess Alexandra's Lady of the Bedchamber, Miss Knollys, would perform this task, unless the number of guests was very few, in which case the Queen would pour the tea. Tea was the fourth meal of the day and when there were no guests, the Queen and Miss Knollys would take it in the conservatory where the Queen would see to some of her correspondence. This room was only ever used when there were no additional guests.

The mistress would ask how the visitor takes their tea, and a separate pot of hot water would have been provided so that she may pour the tea according to the taste of the guest. Milk and sugar were added by the mistress if desired. Milk was always poured in second. To pour the milk in first was not considered acceptable by aristocratic and upper classes, pointed out by Hudson in *Upstairs, Downstairs,* 'Those of us downstairs put the milk in first while those upstairs put the milk in last.'

Offence may be taken if the lady pouring the tea was asked to pour the milk in first; doing so suggesting that the guest doubted the quality of the milk, scalding it by pouring hot water directly on top being a way of killing any bacteria which may be present. Another theory is that if the hostess served tea using fine china, to pour milk in first would lessen the likelihood of the china cracking through the scalding of the liquid; in so doing your guest would see that your china was indeed, fine. Later, when hard-paste porcelain china was introduced to replace its soft-paste predecessor, to show that you were able to afford the superior hard-paste china, you would be seen to pour hot tea in first, proving that the china was of such a high quality that it could take the heat, and also would not to be stained by hot tea. If you poured the milk in first, it was thought that you were lessening the likelihood of the hot tea staining your china, and that it was not therefore of high quality. With hard-paste china being the more up to date version, pouring milk in first is associated with the working classes who were unable to afford it.

In more recent years there have been arguments for and against when to add the milk according to the taste of the tea. It is thought that it tastes softer when the milk is poured in first. Take your pick, from a flavour point of view pour it in first and from snobbery associated with the past, pour it in last!

The particulars at afternoon tea were matters of utmost importance in the Edwardian era. The teaspoon should never be left in the cup and scones or sandwiches should be picked up with three fingers, not five. Holding your little finger up as you drink is a misinterpretation of eleventh-century etiquette that you should hold food with three fingers, not greedily pick it up with five. There followed the freeing of the little finger which somehow lead to its being mistakenly raised to show that it is not being used while eating or drinking. Your little finger should not be uplifted and as you drink tea, you should not look in the eye of your fellow tea drinkers, and nor should you sip your tea from the saucer, a habit adopted by some and considered lowly!

6

From the Other Side of the Coin

My mother used to say, 'You'll need to know all about kitchen stuff and household things because you'll only be able to live if you can work.'

Nancy Jackman with Tom Quinn, *The Cook's Tale*, 2012

It was the task of the servants to ensure that all accessories necessary for the service of tea were put in place. The average middle class home by this period had a servant. Having one showed that you belonged to a successful family. Where only one servant could be afforded, she was a 'maid-of-all-work', a position envied by none. Average-sized houses may have two servants, more if they could afford it.

Domestic writing of the Victorian and Edwardian era states that an average household had eight to ten bedrooms, with a cook, parlour maid, housemaid and a between-maid or 'tweeny'.[65] Live-in servants using up some of the bedrooms, as well as traditionally large families, explain this sizeable household being considered average; it may be argued that 'average' here is being applied to the average household who could afford servants rather than the average person in Britain.

A 'tweeny' would help the housemaid with her duties. Household books advised the mistress to ensure that advantage was not taken with the 'tweeny' being overworked. Dorothy Peel writes of much higher servant numbers in larger houses and stately homes where married servants may live in a house on the estate. The importance of the servants' etiquette was such that entire chapters would be allocated in domestic books to their duties, dress and wages.[66]

Ordering the kitchen supplies was the job of the cook. The few books written by ladies during the Edwardian era advised on allowing 85 g of tea per head per week; this allows for twenty-five to thirty cups per person, showing just how important a role tea played! Tea was served to the family at about 4 o'clock, during which time, while the servants would be on call, the kitchen maid was busy preparing the vegetables for dinner and rustling up the servants' tea for half-past five.

A nest of tea tables, one fitting on top of the other, was used in drawing rooms, tucked away and put out once each day at teatime. They varied in size and height, stacking up one on top of the other; they could be elaborate or plain, depending upon what the hostess could afford. This nest would be discretely put out by a maid with a tablecloth on the largest, on which would be laid the tea in front of the mistress. On one of the tables may be set a spirit lamp over which the tea, coffee or bouillon (meat broth) would be set to ensure it remained hot. Various other tea tables were invented at the time, such as the revolving tea tray, and the 'surprise table'; it held the tea tray in its centre when opened and all signs of the tea would disappear by folding over the wings of the table to conceal the tray, were a servant not at hand to remove it.

Cakes were presented on a curate which was a tiered set of plates within a light wood frame. This would be carried from the top, with three tiers of plates on which the tea edibles were placed. It was made of wood such as mahogany or another wood which would not add too much weight for the servant who carried it. This eventually graduated into silver and china tiered tea trays.

Guests were expected to start at the bottom of the tiered tray with sandwiches (crusts cut off, naturally) and then cakes from the middle tier. The top tier held the hot crumpets, scones, or other baked goods which would be kept warm with a silver dome or fresh tea towel at times. The order of eating the top and middle layer was not important though the sandwiches on the bottom would definitely come first. This order is debated, with bonbons, when served, going at the top, so it remains up to you to decide your own presentation preference. Pretty raised china and silver plates and platters with domes for tea breads would also be used.

The tray set on the mistress's table would carry teacups and saucers, a tea strainer, teaspoons, sugar, preserves, tongs for cubes, a small jug for cream and a small dish containing finely cut slices of lemon for tea with a prong. Teapots, one of fresh tea, one of hot water and any other implement to assist in the service of the tea would also be on the tray. Sugar was added to tea by most, refined white sugar for the rich, the poor using cheaper varieties of sweetener such as molasses, treacle or unrefined brown sugar.[67]

The maid's job was to ensure that the pot of tea would not run dry, and that cups and tea frills such a milk, lemon and sugar were replenished. Members of the family, usually female, would assist in the tea ceremony, and with it happening every day, though a precise art, was not arduous.

Being born into a poor family in the countryside meant that, if your future did not involve working on the land, it would almost certainly be one of service, 'All my childhood, from the earliest day I knew anything, I knew I would have to go into service.'[68] Childhood was cut short with domestic work starting as young as twelve years old. Nancy Jackman records her life in service in *The Cook's Tale*. When dropping her off at work, her father stopped some way before the door, concerned that his daughter's employer may think he thought too highly of himself.

When I was about to leave to live in as a servant I went to see her [mother] and gave her the news. It was the only time I saw her look sad. 'I do hope they will be kind to you,' she said. But she knew, as I did, that for country girls childhood came to an early end.

Insight is given into the viewpoints of servants by accounts written on their behalf, or by mistresses with an empathetic view of those they employed. Diarist and author, Lady Cynthia Asquith wrote that 'no-one from upstairs was required to lend a hand at the sink, not even once a week. Indeed, no such invasion of the Staff's territory would have been tolerated.' This view is shared by Nancy, who worked in service until the 1950s for as long as sixteen hours a day. The presence of her master in the kitchen was not willingly accepted, her finding it an invasion of her space where she felt uncomfortable working in his presence. Any interest shown by employers in the workings of the kitchen was frowned upon by servants who saw the line between upstairs and downstairs as clearly marked; Nancy's father used to say, 'Tuppence ha'penny looking down on tuppence.'

Despite working for the same family for years, never would they be on first name terms. Nancy writes of feeling superior, particularly when considering that

Tea Time by George Goodwin Kilburne (1839–1924). (Courtesy of James Harvey)

many of the privileged ladies knew nothing of changing bed linen or even how to prepare a cup of tea. This was viewed with condescension by the servants. The family of the house in which servants worked who showed occasional interest in the workings of the kitchen were often denounced by the servants. It seems that the regard with which those upstairs were viewed by those downstairs may be a lose-lose situation; Nancy recalls being called upon at 3 a.m. to make hot chocolate after a party she had worked at until midnight, and with her starting again in the early hours! But if the family had no idea how to do it themselves and the servant was not comfortable in showing them, that was the way it would be. The life of a servant was, at times, exhausting.

Of course relationships vary, one example being the three literarily successful Sitwell children whose childhood saw them through the Edwardian era. Their relationship with their parents was not as strong as their relationship with their servants, with whom they were friends for life.[69]

Many left service after the First World War but until then had seen little of what life had to offer outside of the boundaries of village life. Times were changing insofar as servants were fewer, with further opportunities for employment outside of domestic service and subsequent independence holding greater attraction for many.

The Lost Art of Taking Tea

On history's clock it was sunset, and the sun of the old world was setting in a dying blaze of splendour never to be seen again.

Barbara W. Tuchman, quoted by Kate Caffrey, *The 1900s Lady,* 1976

Teatime saw the beginnings of the young lady being able to socialise outside of the home at gatherings known as 'At Homes', under the watchful eye of a chaperone. This graduated into tea dances, or Thés Dansants of the late Victoria and Edwardian era which provided social liberation in daylight hours. Finally women were able to meet with friends, both male and female, soon unhindered by the glances of a chaperon or elderly relative.

Ladies did not eat out until the 1860s when restaurants were opened which had a good reputation. Among the first were the Gaiety, as part of the theatre of the same name, the Holborn and the Criterion. The Waldorf Hotel was renowned for its tea dances around a column of pillars in its white and gold ballroom. A few shillings would gain entry, and dancing would go on from about 3.30 p.m. until 7.30 p.m. with breaks for a cup of tea and an accompanying dainty.

Restaurants and going to the theatre became popular and by the Edwardian era ladies too were allowed to go; when they closed by eleven at night, to continue the night by dancing was not an option considered acceptable for ladies outside of a private house dance. As early as 1912, just one or two of those who dared were seen in nightclubs. Tea Dances and the fashion of going to restaurants and the theatre combined to influence the opening of clubs such as the Cave of the Golden Calf, the Lotus, the Four Hundred, and Murray's. Membership was paid which allowed mothers to remain content that their daughters were not socialising with just any old Tom, Dick and Harry. The outbreak of the First World War saw the wider acceptance of ladies socialising outside of the home alongside the vastly changing roles of women in their contribution to the war effort.

1824 saw men in a coffee shop setting up the foundation of the RSPCA. At this time the House of Lords jeered at the idea of an NSPCC. A woman telephoned the

Baking powder bread (for recipe, see page 76).

police about the plight of an animal being abused next door, knowing very well it was a child, a child being seen legally as the business of its carers. Witnessing such brutality of an innocent highlighted the need for people to look after one another. And so the NSPCC was formed in 1884.[70] Setting up charities gave the country greater insight into a broader spectrum of need.

Death duties introduced in 1894 saw the start of the breaking up of family estates, while taxes imposed by the People's Budget of 1909/10 further affected the wealthy by penalising landowners who were capital rich and often cash poor, or cash poor once the taxes had been paid and they still had an estate to fund. Education, domestic service, the foundation of charities, Window Tax, the Welfare State and the First World War each played a part in the demise of teatime. The 1870 Elementary Education Act began to sow the seeds in women that they may do more outside of the insular world of domestic service and the confines of the family home, furthered in 1880 when attending school between the ages of five and ten became obligatory. Those who would naturally have been expected to work as servants, often in the same house where their parents had worked, began to think beyond this, while those who were expected to be waited on and marry well slowly saw a wider world develop, of which they may become a part.

Working within the estates of the wealthy and privileged had its drawbacks, for both the servers and the served. Expectations of the privileged were high, at times not considering the plight of the working classes, some of whom lived in dire circumstances. The People's Budget aimed to eliminate poverty, put aptly by Lloyd

George, 'a fully-equipped Duke costs as much to keep up as two dreadnoughts (battleships) and was less easy to scrap.'[71]

The Victorian ethos was to provide for those less privileged, yet this did not encompass everyone. There were always those who went without. Tax on the privileged led to the closing of some long-established houses which often provided board and lodging for their servants. No longer were wealthy families able to support such a workforce or to keep their estates running, and so the welfare state took over, as well as helping those in need throughout Britain.

The Edwardian lady and teatime summarised the halcyon days of the Edwardian era. Children came down from their nursery with their nanny, governess or housemaid, girls in white frilly dresses possibly adorned with a string of pearls to have tea with their elders. Servants were informed whether or not their mistresses were 'at home', corsets were loosened, tea dresses were designed, and many young girls looked forward to the day when the art of tea would become theirs. Ladies flirted with men through glances and clandestine meetings. Games were played, their elders looking, gossiping, yet feigning ignorance. A mistress's call would be answered by a housemaid, fires would be lit in bedrooms, carriages waived off with ladies draped in blankets to ensure comfort.

Then in the summer of 1914, relations between England and Germany disintegrated further, the deceased father figure of Edward VII having succeeded in strengthening Britain's European friendships with all but the country of which his nephew, Wilhelm II, was emperor. Five weeks into the summer, Gabriel Princip aimed his revolver at the Austrian heir to the throne, Archduke Franz Ferdinand, and the assassination started the chain reaction that brought war to Britain on 3 August 1914.

Husbands, fathers and other men of fighting age signed up. Women were called upon to assist by working and volunteering to help the war effort. The Voluntary Aid Detachment saw ladies tending to wounded soldiers in large houses which were volunteered as hospitals. Where was the time for regular tea parties and tea dances? The world of the Edwardian lady had changed forever, never to be seen again.

The sight of an Edwardian lady, stepping out of her brougham, her Victoria or Landau outside a Regent street shop was a spectacle which cannot be seen today... The lady swept across the pavement like a Queen, like a procession of one, for she knew how to move and carry herself. She had balance and poise, she had elegance and she was one hundred per cent feminine. She paid no attention to the world around, to the envious glances of her less favoured sisters, but she proceeded like a ship in full sail, a gracious galleon into the harbour of the favoured emporium.[72]

W. Macqueen-Pope, *Goodbye Piccadilly,* 1972

Tablet (for recipe, see page 85).

Recipes

When the white cloth was spread upon the grass, with hot tea and buttered toast and crumpets, a delightfully hungry meal was eaten, and several birds on domestic errands paused to inquire what was going on and were led into investigating crumbs with great activity.

Frances Hodgson Burnett, *The Secret Garden*, 1911

Caraway Seed Cake or Cucumber Sandwich?

Tea parties have been re-embraced in their provision of pleasure and relief from our busy lives of the twenty first century. Rather than the Edwardian teatime of the privileged filling up a day by further opportunity to socialise, gossip or develop romantic relationships, they are seen as a break in our busy lives, whether just a cuppa with a biscuit, or an organised tea party at the weekend. Tea parties and their social, decorative and hedonistic associations are long gone for the vast majority, though surely in most of us, we have a hankering for a snippet of the life of an Edwardian tea-drinker …

In Preparing Tea

First and foremost, a good leaf must be used so as to ensure 'great fragrancy'. Janet McKenzie Hill advises that not heating the teapot by rinsing the inside with boiling water, known as scalding the teapot, before adding the tea leads to a 'bad cup of tea', while neglecting to do so is deemed 'a fatal mistake' by Dorothy Peel.

Scald the teapot and let it become dry and hot. The recommended allowance is one teaspoon of loose-leaf tea per person, and one for the pot. Teabags were discovered by a mistake; often tea was transported in a little bag, and the recipients found it easier to leave it in the bag than to use a tea strainer. The idea caught on, and the first commercial variety of teabags became available in 1904.

However, the adage of one teaspoon of tea leaves per person and one for the pot is questioned by Dorothy Peel, dismissing this as old fashioned. She advises that a better plan is to assess the quality of the tea used as well as the preference of the guests, before deciding how much to add to the pot.73

While teabags had come into existence, they were not yet widely available. It is suggested that tea leaves be added to muslin bags attached to a strong thread, the removal of which should happen when the 'infusion is sufficiently strong'.74 An additional pot containing hot water would accompany the tea pot so that if a guest desired hers weak, her hostess may pour extra water into the cup.

In Preparing Coffee

Coffee should be obtained from only the best coffee berries. These should be kept in tightly shut tins and ground shortly before use, ensuring that the beans are warmed in the oven before grinding.

A Vienna Coffee Machine with a spirit lamp was used in restaurants and deemed preferable in the Edwardian era; coffee machines on the market today are updated versions of this. Viennese coffee shops were renowned for good coffee and excellent service. The popular Austrian novelist, Stephan Zweig, described them as a 'sort of democratic club where people could consume an unlimited number of newspapers and journals'.75 Many a book was written there while coffee would be served, accompanied by snacks, and glasses of water replenished at regular intervals by attentive staff.

To transfer coffee from one pot to another was not recommended, as it causes the coffee to lose heat and fragrance. During a time when appearance was of utmost importance, this posed a serious question for the mind of the discerning hostess. It was advised against using a silver pot to pour the coffee from one container to another, because coffee should be served piping hot; instead the use of a fireproof pot is suggested. Dorothy Peel notes that their less than enticing appearance may be overcome by the purchase of one with gilt rim.76

Coffee was made in a number of ways, some more time-consuming than others. The options are listed below, the most popular of which was the French fashion, Vienna machines being scarcely found within the home. The Turkish fashion is more economical, however, and so both were used.

French Fashion

Requires a percolator, tin or fireproof china. Stand the percolator on the heat and pour boiling water slowly over the coffee. Serve the coffee in the percolator rather than risk losing heat and aroma due to vanity of presentation.

Turkish Fashion

The coffee is placed in a pot and cold water is poured over. Heat the water and coffee up and then allow it to cool a little. Repeat this process twice more. Add a spoonful of cold water to the coffee which allows the sediment to sink to the bottom of the pot. The clear fluid can be poured into cups. The disadvantages of this method are that the temperate will be slightly reduced and there is a possibility of sedimentary material escaping into the clear liquid.

Rough and Ready

Tie the coffee into a muslin bag and place it in a saucepan with cold water. Bring it to the boil. Leftover coffee from the night before, provided it has been kept in a covered pot, may be added to this, and served with milk as a café au lait.

Drinks

Iced Coffee

This recipe is both comforting and delicious in its custardy creaminess. It should be made a few hours in advance to ensure that it is cold. As shown in the picture, this is a delightful accompaniment to Caraway Seed Cake.
Serves 6

Ingredients
300 ml strong coffee
2 tsp sugar
100 ml whole milk
100 ml double cream

Make the coffee and add the sugar immediately so that it melts.

Pour the coffee into a jug and then add the milk and the cream, stirring well.

If serving soon after the coffee is made, surround the jug with ice in a bowl to chill. If it is made in advance, place the jug in the fridge until it is completely cold.

Serve in coffee cups as their small portions are suited to the coffee's richness; these should be chilled in the fridge before serving.

Spiced Tea Syrup

This syrup may be added to tea in place of sugar. It is an exquisite combination which not only infuses your kitchen with the most enticing aroma, but is also a treat for your taste buds.

Ingredients
250 g granulated sugar
250 ml water
1 cinnamon stick
1 tbsp cloves
2 blades mace
½ tbsp allspice berries
Lemon rind

Put the sugar and water in a saucepan over a low heat until a syrup is formed, turning the heat up a little if necessary. Remove the pan from the heat and set aside. Crush the spices lightly in a pestle and mortar or with a rolling pin.
Place the spices in a piece of muslin or similar cooking cloth, and tie a string around the parcel. Put the spice parcel in the syrup over a low heat, allowing the flavour to infuse for a few minutes before moving the pan from the heat.
Pour the syrup into a jar with the spice parcel.
When you are ready to serve, pour some syrup into a bowl with a small ladle and add to your hot drink as desired.

Tea Milk Punch

Egg yolks are added to this drink in a custard-like fashion. Other than eggnog, this type of drink has lost popularity.

Ingredients
1 egg (preferably free range or organic)
3 tbsp caster sugar
¼ cup of thin cream
1 cup of hot, strong tea
2 tsp lemon juice
Grated lemon rind (optional)

Separate the egg white and yolk.
Whisk the egg whites and, when medium peaks are formed, add two spoonfuls of sugar one at a time, combining each thoroughly.
Keep whisking until it is stiff and glossy. The real test is to hold the bowl upside down without the mixture falling out.
Beat the egg yolk together with the remaining sugar, then mix in the cream.
Have ready the cup of tea, and pour this over the mixture, beating the whole time.
Pour into a china bowl or tea cup, and spoon the meringue over the top.
Garnish with the lemon rind, if desired.
Serve with a spoon.

Sandwiches

Egg Sandwiches

This recipes uses both the yolk and the white of the egg in separate sandwich fillings. To start, boil two eggs for 7 minutes and, once cooled, separate the yolks from the whites.

Egg Yolk Filling
2 egg yolks (preferably free range or organic)
25 g very soft butter
Seasoning
Buttered white bread

Mix the yolks with the butter and season to taste.
Spread the mixture on buttered bread and make a sandwich.
Remove the crusts, cut into the desired shape and serve with tea.

Egg White Filling
2 egg whites (preferably free range or organic)
½ tsp mustard powder
¼ tsp salt
80 ml double cream
½ tsp white wine vinegar
Buttered brown bread

In a pan over a medium heat, stir the mustard powder, salt and double cream until well blended.

Slowly add the vinegar, stirring continually until the sauce thickens.

Chop the white of the egg and mix it with some of the dressing until it is of spreading consistency.

Spread on buttered bread and make a sandwich.

Remove the crusts, cut into the desired shape and serve with tea.

Oyster Sandwiches

Oysters were popular, having been the food of the poor until the mid-nineteenth century when the oyster beds dried up and they once again became a food of the rich. Gently poached, and mixed with lemon juice and anchovy essence, they add variety to teatime sandwiches.

Ingredients
Oysters
Lemon
Anchovy Essence
Cayenne pepper or paprika
Buttered brown bread

Shuck the oysters and remove them with their liquor into a small pan. Bring the
oysters to a simmer and poach in the liquor for not much more than a minute.
Transfer the poached oysters to a pestle and mortar. Pound them and mix the meat
with a little lemon and anchovy essence to taste.
Spread the mixture onto the buttered bread and make a sandwich.
Remove the crusts, cut into the desired shape, and serve with tea.

Salmon Sandwiches

Rich and creamy salmon sandwiches are a sumptuous addition to any tea party.

Ingredients
1 tin of salmon (150–200 g)
2 hardboiled egg yolks (preferably free range or organic)
2 tbsp mayonnaise
1 pinch paprika
Buttered bread

Remove any bones from the salmon so that it is smooth and mix with the yolks,
mayonnaise and paprika.
Rub the mixture through a course sieve.
Spread some mixture onto some buttered bread and make a sandwich.
Remove the crusts, cut into the desired shape and serve with tea.

Chicken Cream Sandwiches

Most of us love a chicken sandwich, and gravy or anchovy sauce adds some variety.

Ingredients
200g cooked chicken
3 tbsp cream sauce or mayonnaise
Gravy (optional)
Anchovy essence (optional)
½ tbsp parsley, finely chopped
Buttered bread

Finely chop the chicken and mix it with the cream sauce or mayonnaise. Mix in the gravy or anchovy essence (if using), and the parsley.
Spread onto the buttered bread and make into a sandwich.
Remove the crusts, cut into the desired shape, and serve with tea.

Cucumber Sandwiches

One of the most popular sandwiches; the cucumber must be peeled and thinly sliced. Some sprinkle it with salt and leave for half an hour before patting dry. This ensures that the bread will not be dampened by the moisture if preparing them ahead of time.

Ingredients
Cucumber
Salt
Buttered white bread (use unsalted butter so as the sandwich is not too salty)

Peel the cucumber vertically so that it is stripy. This will add both colour and texture to the sandwich, without having too much texture from possibly tough cucumber skin.
Slice the cucumber very thinly, but not so thin that it does not have some bite to it.
Lay the cucumber slices in a single layer onto the bottom slice of buttered bread.
Sprinkle the cucumber lightly with salt.
Add the buttered top slice, remove the crusts, cut into the desired shape and serve with tea.

Onion Sandwiches

An unusual sandwich filling which is delicious, provided it is spread thinly.

Ingredients
1 sweet onion
1 tbsp mayonnaise
1 tsp anchovy essence
Fresh parsley, finely chopped
Buttered bread

Grate the onion and mix it with the mayonnaise and anchovy essence, adding more or less according to taste.

Spread the mixture thinly on the buttered bread, garnishing with parsley if you wish. Make a sandwich, remove the crusts, cut into the desired shape and serve with tea.

Nasturtium Sandwiches

So pretty and fresh, these will suit any summer tea party.

Ingredients
Nasturtium leaves
Mayonnaise
Buttered white bread

Butter the bread, then take a biscuit cutter slightly smaller than the nasturtium leaves and cut circles of bread.

Place a leaf on top of the bread circles and a small blob of mayonnaise.

Top with another of bread and repeat for however many leaves you have.

Decorate the plate with nasturtium flowers (these can also be eaten).

Chequer Board Sandwiches

This is a way of presenting the sandwiches in small squares like a chequer board. Use brown and white bread with whichever fillings you choose, and arrange. Simple and effective.

Biscuits

Goosnargh Cake

These biscuits were made at the end of the sewing of wheat in spring. While the origin of the recipe is unknown, around Whitsuntide, they were produced in their thousands. Caraway was a popular addition to cakes and pastries. Goosnargh cake's similarity to shortbread makes it a suitable tea-time accompaniment. *Makes 14–16.*

Ingredients
200 g unsalted butter
50 g caster sugar
1 ½ tbsp caraway seeds
½ tsp ground coriander
300 g plain flour
Extra caster sugar for sprinkling

Preheat the oven to 150°C.
Cream the butter and sugar together until light and fluffy, then mix in the caraway seeds and the coriander.
Add the flour, incorporating it fully, but stop mixing as soon as it is combined.
Roll the mixture on a lightly floured surface and use a 6 cm pastry cutter to form smooth rounds.

Lay the rounds on a baking tray and sprinkle each one with caster sugar.
Leave them to rest in a cool place for at least two hours. This helps form a crust of sugar and allows the flavour to infuse into the biscuit.
Bake for 20 minutes or until cooked through.
Leave to cool on the tray before transferring to a wire rack.
Serve with tea.

Shrewsbury Biscuits

> Measure not my love by substance of it, which is brittle, but by the form of it which is circular.
>
> Lord Herbert of Cherbury, 1602

Renowned as biscuits eaten by country folk, Shrewsbury biscuits were made with varying additions such as cinnamon, nutmeg and rosewater. The essence is in the flour to butter ratio, ensuring their crispness. Without the egg, they will be more brittle.
Makes 10–12

Ingredients
100 g unsalted butter
100 g caster sugar
1 egg (preferably free range or organic) (optional)
1 tsp rosewater (add another tsp if you are keen on rosewater)
Grated rind of unwaxed lemon
55 g currants
200 g plain flour

Cream the butter and sugar together until light and fluffy and then combine the remaining ingredients.
Roll the dough out onto a lightly floured surface and cut the biscuits into circles with a 6 cm pastry cutter. Place the biscuits on a non-stick baking tray, and refrigerate for 20 minutes.
Preheat the oven to 180°C.
Bake for 8 minutes.
Allow to cool on a wire rack.
Serve with tea.

Grantham Gingerbread

There are several varieties of ginger bread, or ginger biscuits, this being among the most popular. Produced as early as the 1800s, in the Edwardian era they remained popular. They have a crisp snap and are reminiscent of Yuletide.
Makes 25 biscuits

Ingredients
100 g unsalted butter
200 g caster sugar
1 ½ tbsp ground ginger
200 g plain flour

Cream the butter, caster sugar and ginger together until light and fluffy.
Add the flour, mixing in thoroughly.
Put the mixture onto clingfilm, wrap it up in the shape of a cylinder and refrigerate for 20 minutes. It can be made in advance and removed from the fridge 20 minutes before slicing.
Preheat the oven to 180°C.
After 20 minutes have passed, remove the clingfilm, take a sharp knife and cut the cylinder into thin biscuits, placing them on a non-stick baking tray.
Bake for 8 minutes or until browned.
Remove from the oven and leave on the baking tray for a further 2 minutes before transferring to a wire rack.
Serve with tea.

Afternoon Tea Biscuits

These are light and delicate. Butter pats are surplus to requirement but if you are lucky enough to find some lurking in your attic, use them to shape the biscuits. Otherwise, this wonderfully unsticky mixture is easy to shape with floured bare hands.

Makes 20 biscuits

Ingredients

110 g unsalted butter at room temperature
220 g caster sugar
2 eggs (preferably free range or organic)
½ tsp vanilla extract
220 g cornflour
220 g plain flour
Jam

Preheat the oven to 170°C.
Cream the butter and sugar together, whisk the eggs and add them with vanilla to the mixture, followed by a tablespoon of the flour to stop the mixture splitting.
Mix in both types of flour and form into flat biscuits, about half a centimetre high. They should be about 3 or 4 cm in diameter.
Place on non-stick baking trays. If the mixture is soft, put the trays in the fridge for 20 minutes or so to firm up.

Bake for 6 minutes, turning the biscuits over for an additional couple of minutes to ensure they are crisp.

Remove from the oven onto a wire rack. While they are still warm, place half a teaspoonful of jam between two biscuits and press lightly together.

Serve with tea.

Petticoat Tails

In the twelfth century these biscuits were named after their likeness to the frilly edges of petticoats. The method of mixing the shortbread paste ensures a light texture.

Serves 8

Ingredients
300 g plain flour
75 g caster sugar, plus extra for sprinkling
200 g butter, diced into small cubes

Preheat the oven to 200°C.

Put the flour and sugar in a mixer or bowl and add the butter.

Mix them together by lifting the mixture up and crumbling between your fingers, so that it resembles breadcrumbs.

Press the contents of the bowl together.

If it is warm, cover with clingfilm and leave the mixture in the fridge to firm up for 20 minutes before rolling and shaping.

If the mixture is cool enough, using a little extra flour, roll it out into a 20 cm round. Scallop the edges with your thumb and index finger, using a little flour to help if necessary. Make a pattern using the prongs of a fork on the surface and, with a knife, mark out 8 sections.

Place in the fridge for 20 minutes, then bake for 15 minutes or until cooked through. If it is not cooked after 15 minutes, then turn off the oven and leave the door open a little, for it to crisp up. Be careful to watch the colour so that it does not darken too much.

Let it cool on a wire rack and sprinkle with extra caster sugar if you like.

Serve whole so that its decoration may be appreciated, with a cup of tea.

Lemon Tarts

Leftover pastry was used to make little tarts which would be filled with jam, desiccated coconut, cream and sugar, or whatever was at hand. These tarts are delicious as they are or topped with meringue.

Makes 24

Ingredients
Pastry:
300 g plain flour
150 g unsalted butter
1 tbsp caster sugar
2 egg yolks (preferably free range or organic)
Whole milk

Lemon Curd:
160mls lemon juice
120g caster or granulated sugar
100g unsalted butter
4 eggs (preferably free range or organic)

Meringue (optional):
120 ml egg white (preferably free range or organic)
200g caster sugar

You will need a 6 or 7 cm pastry cutter, and a tartlet tin.

Preheat the oven to 200°C.
Mix together the pastry ingredients and add a little milk if it does not come together. The less liquid added, the lighter the pastry will be.
Wrap it in cling film and put it in the fridge while you make the curd.
Put all of the ingredients for the curd in a pan over a low heat, stirring gently until it thickens.
Remove from the heat and sieve into a bowl. Cover and set aside.
Take the pastry from the fridge and roll thinly on a floured surface.
Cut 6 or 7 cm circles of pastry and arrange in the tartlet tin, filling gaps with pastry where necessary.
Line each tartlet with baking paper or a petit-four case, and fill with baking beans.
(An alternative is to fill the uncooked pastry with the curd before baking. Whereas the shine of the curd will be lost, this avoids pre-baking the pastry.)
Bake for 5–8 minutes until cooked through.
If you have not cooked the tartlets with the filling, remove the baking beans and paper and add the curd to the tartlet cases when they are hot.
Cool and serve as they are, or go to the next step to add a meringue topping.
Whisk the egg whites and when medium peaks are formed, add the sugar, spoonful by spoonful, and keep whisking until it is stiff and glossy. The real test is to hold the bowl upside down without the mixture falling out.
Pipe the meringue on top of the pastry.
Place under a flame or grill until lightly browned.

Cakes and Breads

Scones

There is nothing new about scones, but a tea book without them may be questioned. This recipe is unadulterated, but do add a tablespoon of sugar for a sweeter scones, or cheese for a savoury version. The Edwardians would have served these warm, under a dome or towel on a 3-tiered curate or tea plate.
Makes 8

Ingredients
300 g self-raising flour
70 g unsalted butter
Pinch of salt
200 ml whole milk

Preheat the oven to 200°C.
Rub together the flour, butter and salt so that the mixture resembles breadcrumbs.
Stir in the milk slowly, until you have a mixture which is well combined, but not sticky. Do not over mix.

Lightly scatter some flour on a surface and roll out the mixture until it is about 3 cm high. Cut the scones with a cutter, whichever size you wish and place them on a baking tray.
Bake for 20 minutes or until light to lift.
Cool on a wire rack and serve with butter, cream and jam, and of course tea.

Borrowdale Tea Bread

This is a plain fruit bread, so named, it is thought, because the fruit added to it has been soaked in tea.

Ingredients
100 g raisins
100 g currants
250 ml tea
400 g self-raising flour

Put the fruit in a bowl and cover with the tea.
After a few hours, drain the fruit over a bowl to keep the liquid.
Preheat the oven to 180°C.
Put the flour in a bowl and add the fruit, mixing in about 150mls of the reserved tea until the mixture is of dropping consistency.
Transfer the mixture into a greased or lined loaf tin and bake for 40 minutes, or until a skewer inserted into the centre of the loaf comes out clean.
Set the loaf onto a wire rack to cool and serve sliced, with butter.

Devonshire Split

These are also known as Chudleighs, and a larger version is known as a Cornish Split. Used in place of scones at cream teas, these are a rich and soft bun made with cream, sometimes milk, instead of water. Each bun is split and a filled with a dollop of cream and a spoonful of jam.
Makes 14

Ingredients
400 g strong white bread flour
7g sachet dried yeast
20 g caster sugar
20 g butter, softened
300 ml cream
Jam and whipped cream for serving

Put the flour, yeast, sugar and butter in a bowl.
Warm the cream to a tepid temperature and pour it on top of the ingredients in the bowl, mixing with a knife.
Knead for 10 minutes, or 5 minutes, if using a mixer with a dough hook.
Cover the bowl with a tea towel and leave for an hour.
During this time, preheat the oven to 200°C.
Take a piece of dough (roughly the size of a golf ball) and form it into a smooth ball by folding it over itself until you have a smooth surface. Place on a non-stick baking tray.
Repeat this until you have finished the mixture.
Leave the dough to rise for half an hour or until the buns have doubled in size.
Bake for 20 minutes and then remove onto a wire rack to cool.
Once cool, put a slit in the bun as if you were making a sandwich but not cutting it completely in half because the bun needs to remain in one piece.
Add a large spoonful of whipped cream and a teaspoonful of jam on top.
Serve and indulge.

Ripon Spice Cake

Originally this recipe used yeast, until baking powder became more widely available in the Edwardian era. Using lard produces a crumbly texture, with spices and dried fruit more commonly used a century ago.
Serves 10

Ingredients
250 g plain flour
3 tsp baking powder
50 g lard, diced into small cubes
50 g unsalted butter, diced into small cubes
200 g brown sugar
1 tsp mace or cinnamon
½ tsp cinnamon
80 g currants
80 g raisins
50 g walnuts
80 ml milk

Preheat the oven to 160°C.

Put the flour and baking powder in a bowl and add the lard and butter.

Rub the mixture with your fingers until it resembles breadcrumbs.

Mix in the spices and then add the remaining ingredients, apart from the milk.

Use the milk to combine the mixture until it drops easily from the spoon.

Transfer to a greased or lined loaf tine and bake for 1 hour.

Cool on a wire rack.

Serve as it is or with butter.

Eccles Cakes

Eccles cakes go as far back as 1769 when Mrs Raffald's recipe involved calf foot meat combined with apples, oranges, nutmeg, egg yolk, currants and brandy, called mincemeat. This was adapted to exclude the meat, made in Eccles and sold in James Birch's shop in 1793. Although less common today, during the Edwardian era these were very popular, one likely reason being that they kept well, which may be put down to the addition of brandy. These are both irresistible and simple to make.
Makes 4

Ingredients
40 g unsalted butter
½ tsp cinnamon
200 g currants
50g brown sugar
200 g puff pastry
1 egg white, beaten (preferably free range or organic)
Caster sugar for sprinkling

Preheat the oven to 200°C.

Melt the butter and mix in the cinnamon, currants and sugar.

For each cake, roll out 50 g of pastry to about 14cm in diameter and pile the currant mixture on top. Fold over the pastry, encapsulating the currants. Secure by squeezing the sides of the pastry together, adding a little water if necessary.

Put the cakes on a baking tray with the sealed edges underneath. Press them down with a rolling pin or the palm of your hand.

Brush both sides with egg white and sprinkle the cakes with caster sugar. Make a couple of slits in the middle of the top side of the cakes. Spray lightly with water to caramelise the cakes when baking (a spray bottle for plants works perfectly).

Bake for 8 minutes and then briefly remove them, pressing them down with a spatula. Liquid will run out which is beneficial to the end result. Eccles cakes are not supposed to puff up, hence the need to flatten them.

Return the cakes to the oven for another 5 minutes or until they are golden and sticky. Remove from the oven onto a cooling rack.

They will keep for a few days, and are particularly good served warm with a cup of tea.

Treacle and Walnut or Raisin Bread

A little like a malt loaf, this is a dense bread, served spread with butter.

Ingredients
275 g self-raising flour
75 g brown sugar
3 tbsp treacle
50 g raisins or chopped walnuts
1 egg (preferably free range or organic)
120 ml whole milk

Preheat the oven to 190°C.
Put the flour, sugar, treacle and the raisins or walnuts into a mixing bowl.
In a separate bowl, whisk the egg into the milk and stir into the treacle mixture.
When well combined, transfer the mixture to a greased or lined loaf tin.
Bake for 40 minutes or until a skewer inserted into the centre comes out clean.
Turn out onto a cooling rack after 5 minutes.
Serve with tea.

Dough Cakes

The dough recipe that follows is divided in two, one half for the Caraway Sultana Dough Cake, the other half for the Demerara and Currant Dough cake.

Ingredients
500 g strong white bread flour
7 g sachet dried yeast
1 tsp salt
1 tbsp plain oil or butter
1 egg, whisked (preferably free range or organic)
250 ml tepid water

Put all of the ingredients except the water in a mixing bowl.
Pour in the water, stirring with a knife until the ingredients combine. You may need more or less water.
Knead for 10 minutes, 5 minutes if using a mixer with a dough hook, until smooth.
Cover the dough in a bowl with a tea towel and allow it to rise for 1 ½–2 hours.

Caraway Sultana Dough Cake

This is possibly my favourite, reminiscent of flavours associated with Scandinavia, and a forgotten part of British history.

Ingredients
Half the dough from the dough recipe
80 g clarified dripping or lard
90 g brown sugar
90 g sultanas
3 tsp caraway seeds

Lay the dough out on a lightly floured surface in a rectangular shape, roughly the size of an A4 piece of paper. Sprinkle the remaining ingredients over the surface, dotting the lard around.

Roll it up like a jam roly-poly and then fold each end over and keep folding until you feel that the ingredients are evenly spread. Try to avoid the filling poking through the surface. Place the mixture in a greased or lined loaf tin and leave to rise for 1 hour. During this time, preheat the oven to 200°C.

Bake for 20–25 minutes, then cool on a wire rack.

Serve sliced with jam, if you like, and tea.

Demerara and Currant Dough Cake

Rather like a light Dorset lardy cake but made with butter, this is both indulgent and very good.

Ingredients
Half the dough from the dough recipe
50 g butter, diced into small cubes
110 g demerara sugar
110 g sultanas, raisins or currants
30 g candied peel (optional)

Lay the dough out on a lightly floured surface in a rectangular shape, roughly the size of an A4 piece of paper. Sprinkle the remaining ingredients over the surface, dotting the butter around.

Roll it up like a jam roly-poly and then fold each end over and keep folding until you feel that the ingredients are evenly spread.

Place the mixture in a greased or lined loaf tin and leave to rise for 1 hour. During this time, preheat the oven to 200°C.

Bake for 20–25 minutes, then cool on a wire rack.

Served sliced with tea.

Sally Lunns

Solange Luyon came to Bath, it is said, in 1680, escaping persecution in France. The locals couldn't pronounce her name and so it morphed into Sally Lunn, the name which was then given to the buns she used to make. Although the exact recipe is kept secret, these are very similar, and should be lighter than a brioche and creamier than a standard bun. *Makes 8 small buns or 1 loaf*

Ingredients
200 ml whole milk
80 g unsalted butter
400 g plain flour
½ tsp salt
40g caster sugar
7 g sachet dried yeast

Warm the milk in a small pan and melt the butter in it. Put the flour, salt, sugar and yeast into a mixing bowl. When the milk is lukewarm, pour it and the butter into the dry ingredients, stirring the mixture together with a knife.
Knead for 10 minutes, 5 minutes if using a mixer with a dough hook.
Cover the bowl with a tea towel and allow the mixture to rise for 1 ½–2 hrs.
On a lightly floured surface, roll out the dough into a rectangular shape. Form into buns about 3 cm high and lay them onto baking trays, keeping them spaced well apart.
Leave again for up to an hour; they will almost double in size.
During this time, preheat the oven to 200°C.
Bake for 8–10 minutes and allow to cool on a wire rack.
Serve toasted and buttered with a cup of tea.

Baking Powder Bread

If teatime arrives and there is nothing to have with tea, this loaf may be made in haste. It is crumbly and surprisingly hard to resist (picture on page 48).

Ingredients
450 g plain flour
4 tsp baking powder
1 tsp salt
25 g butter, softened
250 ml whole milk

Preheat the oven to 180°C.
Mix the flour, baking powder, salt and butter together, and then pour in the milk, mixing with a knife as you do so.
When it is well combined, transfer the mixture to a greased or lined loaf tin.
Bake for 30 minutes and remove onto a wire rack to cool.
Serve warm with butter, jam and of course, tea.

Tea Cakes

Tea cakes are synonymous with teatime comfort. These are light and amazingly delicious homemade treats.

Makes 6–8

Ingredients
200 ml whole milk
25 g unsalted butter
500 g strong white flour
7 g sachet dried yeast
½ tsp salt
40 g sugar
2 tsp mixed spice or cinnamon
125 g sultanas, raisins, and a little mixed peel (optional)

Warm the milk until it is lukewarm, and add the butter.
Put the flour, yeast, salt, sugar and spices into a mixing bowl, and pour the milk and butter onto the mixture, stirring all the time.

Knead for 10 minutes, 5 minutes if using a mixer with a dough hook.

Cover the bowl with a tea towel and set it aside to rise for 1 ½–2 hours.

Lay the dough out on a lightly floured surface in a rectangular shape, roughly the size of an A4 piece of paper. Sprinkle the fruit on top, then roll it up like a jam roly-poly and fold and push until the fruit is evenly dispersed.

Cut with a round cutter into buns about 2.5 cm high.

Lay the buns on a baking sheet and leave them to rise for 30 minutes.

During this time, preheat the oven to 200°C.

Bake for 10 minutes or until the buns sound hollow when tapped on the base.

Cool on a wire rack.

Serve toasted with butter and tea.

Pikelets

Rather like a crumpet, but very speedily made without a mould, these are light and delicious. In Edwardian times, they would be kept warm and served under a dome, whether at the top of a tiered tea tray, or on a plate, as featured in the photograph. While this can be used immediately after the mixture is made, like pancake batter it can also be made in advance. Leaving it to rest allows for a more tender texture.
Makes 10-12

Ingredients
200 g self-raising flour
10 g caster sugar
25 g very soft butter, plus extra for the pan
1 egg (preferably free range or organic)
250 ml whole milk

Put the flour, sugar and butter in a mixing bowl. Whisk the egg and milk together before pouring in, mixing thoroughly. Set the batter aside until needed, keeping it in the fridge if this will be longer than 30 minutes.
Heat a pan and melt some butter. When it sizzles, pour a round of the batter onto the butter, as if making drop scones.
When bubbles form on the surface, turn them over and allow to cook through for a minute or so on the other side.
Serve with butter and jam or honey, and tea or milk, as children adore these.

Caraway Seed Cake

In recent years this delicious cake has lost its popularity. My great-grandfather loved it, as did many Edwardians, both for its taste and perhaps the refreshing digestive qualities associated with the caraway seed. It is less sweet than your average cake, with a grown-up caraway flavour. Mace and nutmeg were usually also added to cakes at this time, and it is delicious served with iced coffee (recipe and picture on page 53)

Ingredients
250 g unsalted butter
175 g caster sugar
3 eggs (preferably free range or organic)
250 g self-raising flour
4 tbsp caraway seeds
50 ml whole milk (Mrs Beeton recommends using Madeira or brandy instead)
Demerara sugar for sprinkling

Preheat the oven to 180°C.
Cream the butter and sugar together until light and fluffy. Mix in the eggs one at a time, each with a spoonful of flour to stop the mixture curdling.
Stir in the remaining flour and the caraway seeds with the milk (or Madeira or brandy), adding as much as you need for dropping consistency.
Pour into a greased or lined 18–20 cm high-sided cake tin. Sprinkle with demerara sugar.
Bake for 45 minutes or until a skewer inserted into the centre comes out clean.
Remove the cake from the oven and leave it in the tin. After 5 minutes remove from the tin onto a wire rack.
Best served warm shortly after baking, with iced coffee.

Madeira Cake

In the seventeenth century, when dinner was served earlier, cake was sometimes eaten at midday instead of lunch with an alcoholic drink such as Madeira. The cake is named because of the popularity of serving it with Madeira. There are two secrets for success: use free range or organic eggs whose yolks will contribute a beautiful yellow to the cake; and cover it while baking and cooling. Covering the cake will not produce the split on the surface, for which Madeira cakes are renowned, but will produce a moist cake.

Ingredients
175 g unsalted butter
175 g golden caster sugar (or standard caster sugar)
3 eggs (preferably free range or organic)
200 g flour
50 ml milk
Grated rind of a lemon (optional)
Demerara sugar for sprinkling

Preheat the oven to 160°C

Cream the butter and sugar together until light and fluffy. Mix in the eggs one at a time, each with a spoonful of flour to stop them curdling.

Add the remaining flour and mix in, followed by the milk until the mixture falls from the spoon easily.

Transfer the mixture to a greased or line 18–20 cm cake tin. Surround the tin loosely in baking paper, securing it at the base of the tin, using its weight to hold the paper in place. Sprinkle with demerara sugar.

Bake for 1 hour or until a skewer inserted into the centre comes out clean.

Re-cover the cake with the baking paper and leave it for a few hours or until the next day. This ensures a soft top and a moist, light, buttery cake.

Serve with Madeira, or tea.

Ices

Queen Victoria was particularly fond of ice cream, in which only the privileged few who had an ice cave could indulge. In the Edwardian era, when refrigeration was becoming slightly more common, it became available for more (though still privileged) people. Condensed milk was often used in place of fresh cream. The idea was to serve ices from a bowl surrounded with ice at summer tea parties.

Peach Melba

Invented in the early 1890s by Auguste Escoffier, the chef at the Savoy Hotel in London, Peach Melba was both created and named for the Australian opera singer, Nellie Melba.

Serves 8

Ingredients
3 egg yolks (preferably free range or organic)
100 g caster sugar
1 tbsp cornflour
1 tsp vanilla essence (optional)
500 ml whole milk
250 ml cream or condensed milk (if you use condensed milk, do not add sugar. The result will be sweet enough without)
8 peach halves
8 tbsp raspberry sauce
Whipped cream (optional)

Cream together the eggs, sugar, cornflour and vanilla essence until light and pale. Heat the milk, and pour on top of the mixture, stirring all the time.

Over a low heat, or in a bowl set over simmering water, stir the mixture until it has thickened, coating the back of a wooden spoon. Mix in the evaporated milk, double cream or condensed milk. (This is the ice cream custard referred to in the next recipe.) Pour into an ice cream machine to freeze or place in a container in the freezer and beat every 20 minutes until it is too stiff to do.

Place a scoop of ice cream in a bowl, with half a peach on top and some raspberry sauce, topped with cream if you wish.

You may like to add 2 tbsp of brandy or any other liqueur.

Strawberry and Other Fruit Ice

Edwardian recipe books contain further variations on ices. Use the custard base such as that used for the vanilla ice cream above, but substitute the vanilla for other flavours.

Ingredients
800 ml ice cream custard (from above recipe)
800 ml fruit puree, sweetened to taste (bearing in mind that ice cream requires a higher sugar content than dishes served at warm temperatures)

Combine the ingredients and taste, adding more sugar if necessary.

Pour into an ice cream machine to freeze or place in a container in the freezer and beat every 20 minutes until it is too stiff to do so.

Bonbons

Chocolate Mints

These taste more like After Eight mints than Bendicks Bittermints. Don't be put off if they're not pretty, they will still be delicious.

Ingredients
1 egg white (preferably free range or organic)
2 tsp mint extract
250 g icing sugar
125 g dark chocolate

Whisk the egg white and essence in a bowl and sift the icing sugar into it, a little at a time. The amount of icing sugar needed will depend on the size of the egg white so this amount is not precise.

When the mixture is well combined, roll it into a cylinder and wrap it in cling film. Place it in the freezer for 20 minutes or so until it is firm and easy to shape.

Break up the chocolate and melt in a heat-proof bowl over a pan of simmering water.

When the chocolate has melted, remove the mint paste from the freezer and cut into slices. These should be pastel-shaped.

Dip the mints into the chocolate and carefully put them on a baking tray.

Set aside in a cool place until ready to serve (avoid the fridge as you may get fridge burn – white marks on the chocolate).

Butterscotch

Crunchy and delicious, this goes very well at the top of a tiered tea tray with, shortbread on the second tier.

Ingredients
250 g sugar (this can be part brown, part caster, or raw golden caster sugar)
90 ml water
1 tsp lemon juice
60 ml double cream

Prepare a baking tray, greased or lined with baking paper.
Put the sugar and water in a pan over a low heat. Once melted, turn the heat up and bring to boil, using a sugar thermometer.
When it reaches 116°C, stir in the lemon juice and then the cream. It will splutter so stand back. Stir in the mixture so that it does not burn.
When it reaches 135°C remove it from the heat, pour onto the baking tray and allow to cool.
After a few minutes, mark out squares with a sharp knife.
When it has cooled, cut or break the hardened mixture and enjoy with shortbread, tea, or crushed up and scattered on ice cream.

Tablet

Sweet and irresistible, tablet was commonly made as a bonbon, especially where unsweetened condensed milk, which we now call evaporated milk, was easily procurable. This is based on a French Canadian recipe called *Sucre à la Crème*. My great-great aunt in Canada kept a jar of it on her mantle piece. The recipe is the same as tablet, but uses brown sugar.

Ingredients
750 g brown or caster sugar
350 ml double cream or evaporated milk
125 g unsalted butter

Place the sugar and cream or evaporated milk in a heavy based pan over a low heat, until small bubbles appear on the surface, at which point the sugar has melted. This should take about 20 minutes.

Turn up the heat, but not too much, and gradually bring the mixture to the boil until it reaches 127°C on a sugar thermometer, stirring now and then as it may catch on the bottom of the pan. It is especially important to stir it if you use evaporated milk. If it does catch, you can sieve it after adding the butter and before whisking.

It is much easier to use a sugar thermometer but if you do not have one, test that it is ready by putting a small teaspoonful of the mixture onto a cool plate. If it solidifies, it is ready.

Remove from the heat and add the butter, beating it in. With an electric whisk beat the mixture for another 30 seconds. Pour it onto some baking paper and allow to set. Serve with tea or crumbled on ice cream.

Acknowledgements

Rather like my first book, this has been another solitary experience, though without the historical links my husband Ants found, I would not have been able to produce it to a set deadline. Testing the recipes has been done via coffee mornings and my two children who have been very willing taste testers!

The perfect light in our home is on the floor by a windowed door. Photo shoots have therefore taken place rather hurriedly with dogs lurking in the background, or lying in their adjacent basket, ready to leap on the carefully spread tablecloth and beautiful china. With these canine risk factors at large and a doting owner, the only way to accomplish both unhindered and abundant tea table shots has been to bake a few dishes at once! So we have certainly had an extravaganza of teatime treats.

Enormous thanks must go to James and Flora Harvey for use of the late Christopher Wood's Edwardian painting collection. Flora is a school friend, James her art-dealer husband who was left the painting rights by Christopher, and Christopher was a childhood family friend so between them serendipity has played its part.

Richard Powers of Stanford University's Dance Division in America has allowed the use of some beautiful photographs and illustrations from the Edwardian era to which the book owes huge thanks.

This has been an interesting project with a personal culinary gain. Thank you to Amberley for the idea, and thank you to our predecessors of the Edwardian era for their inspiration.

Notes

1. Jane Pettigrew, *A Social History of Tea*, 2001 p. 02
2. www.tea.co.uk/a-social-history
3. www.tea.co.uk/catherine-of-braganza
4. www.tea.co.uk/a-social-history
5. Pettigrew, p. 12
6. Pettigrew, p. 150
7. www.tea.co.uk/east-india-company
8. www.smuggling.co.uk/gazetteer_se_16.html
9. www.tea.co.uk/tea-smuggling
10. John Jeffrey Cook, *William Pitt and his Taxes*, 2010
11. www.theguardian.com/uk/2007/feb/04/schools.education1
12. britishfood.about.com/od/faq/f/highteavafttea.htm
13. www.theguardian.com/books/2012/dec/14/bee-wilson-rereading-food-england-hartley
14. www.edwardianpromenade.com/amusements/eaters-of-dreams/
15. Kate Caffrey, *The 1900s Lady*, 1976, p. 26
16. www.edwardianpromenade.com/royalty/the-amorous-life-of-edward-vii/
17. Caffrey, p. 21
18. Elinor Gwyn, *Three Weeks*, 1907
19. Caffrey, p. 66
20. Caffrey, p. 23
21. Pettigrew, p. 115
22. www.janeaustensworld.wordpress.com/tag/edwardian-era/
23. Mrs C. S. Peel, *How to Keep House*, 1906, p. 190
24. Peel, *How to Keep House*, p. 112
25. www.edwardianpromenade.com/etiquette/the-etiquette-of-social-calls-and-calling-cards/
26. Mrs C. S. Peel, *Life's Enchanted Cup, An Autobiography 1872-1933*, 1933, p. 98

27. Peel, *How to Keep House*, p. 141
28. *Anne of Green Gables*
29. Caffrey, p. 67
30. Pettigrew, p. 12
31. Pettigrew, p. 120
32. Joanne Olian, *Victorian and Edwardian Fashions from 'La Mode Illustrée'*, 1998
33. Philippe Perrot, *Fashioning the Bourgeoisie* (translated by Richard Bienvenu), 1994, seen in Joanne Olian, *Victorian and Edwardian Fashions from 'La Mode Illustrée'*, 1998
34. en.wikipedia.org/wiki/Effects_of_tight_lacing_on_the_body
35. Caffrey, p. 16
36. Peel, *Life's Enchanted Cup,* p. 46
37. Caffrey, p. 16
38. Daisy Ashford, The Young Visiters, 1919
39. Caffrey, p. 17
40. Caffrey, p. 19
41. Caffrey, p. 51
42. Beatrice Crozier, *The Tango and How to Dance it*
43. Caffrey, p. 114
44. 'Free and Easy Manners in London Society'. Evening Post, Volume XVII, Issue 387, 5 April 1879, p. 5
45. www.edwardianpromenade.com/dance/tango-teas-and-tangocitis/
46. www.edwardianpromenade.com/category/dance/
47. Jane Pettigrew, *Waltz Around a Tea Table* http://www.teamuse.com/article_010702.html
48. Phyllis E. Tortora and Chris Eubank, *Survey of Historic Costume*, p. 421
49. Joanne Olian, *Victorian and Edwardian Fashions from 'La Mode Illustrée'*, 1998, p. viii
50. Olian, p. ix
51. www.socialdance.stanford.edu/syllabi/19th_century.htm
52. Mrs C. S. Peel, *Still Room Cookery*, 1905, p. 8
53. Peel, *Still Room Cookery,* p. 8
54. Robert Edward Norton: Secret Germany: Stefan George and his Circle
55. Peel, *Still Room Cookery*, p. 10
56. www.history.co.uk/study-topics/history-of-london/londons-coffee-houses
57. www.history.co.uk/study-topics/history-of-london/londons-coffee-houses
58. Thomas Short, *Discourses on Tea, Sugar, Milk, Made-Wines, Spirits, Punch, Tobacco*, 1750
59. www.tea.co.uk
60. www.tea.co.uk/tea-smuggling.
61. Pettigrew, p. 103
62. www.edwardianpromenade.com/food/an-edwardian-breakfast/
63. Caffrey, p. 50

64. Caffrey, p. 11
65. Caffrey, p. 19
66. Peel, *How to Keep House*, p. 113
67. Peel, *How to Keep House,* p. 113
68. Peel, *Life's Enchanted Cup*, p.96
69. Peel, *How to Keep House*
70. Peel, *How to Keep House*
71. Pettigrew, p. 56
72. Nancy Jackman with Tom Quinn, *The Cook's Tale*, 2012, p. 19
73. Caffrey, p.52
74. Peel, *Life's Enchanted Cup,* p.144
75. en.wikipedia.org/wiki/

Bibliography

Asquith, Lady Cynthia, *Remember and Be Glad,* 1952
Caffrey, Kate, *The 1900s Lady,* 1976
Forster, E. M., *Howard's End,* 1910
Forster, E. M., *A Room with a View,* 1908
Hartley, Dorothy, *Food in England,* 1954
Jackman, Nancy with Tom Quinn, *The Cook's Tale,* 1912
Maloney, Alison, *Life Below Stairs,* 2011
Mason, Laura with Catherine Brown, *Traditional Foods of Britain,* 1999
Montgomery, Lucy Maud, *Anne of Green Gables,* 1908
Peel, Mrs C. S., *How to Keep House,* 1906
Peel, Mrs C. S., *Life's Enchanted Cup, An Autobiography 1872–1933,* 1933
Peel, Mrs C. S., *My Own Cookery Book,* 1923
Peel, Mrs C. S., *Still Room Cookery,* 1905
Pettigrew, Jane, *A Social History of Tea,* 2001

About the Author

Vicky Straker's love of Edwardian cooking was inspired by her great-great grandmother, Dorothy Peel, who set up the Daily Mail Food Bureau in 1918 and taught millions of women to cook during the war. Dorothy's recipe for Afternoon Tea biscuits is included in this book. Vicky is also the author of *Bicycles, Bloomers and Rationing Recipes – The Life and Times of Dorothy Peel OBE.*

Also available from Amberley Publishing

Vanessa Berridge

The Princess's Garden

Royal Intrigue and the Untold Story of Kew

Also available from Amberley Publishing

Tea

A Very British
Beverage

Paul Chrystal

Available from all good bookshops or to order direct
Please call **01453–847–800**
www.amberley-books.com